CALIFORNIA WRITERS CLUB

FOUNDED IN 1909

THE
2020
LITERARY REVIEW

AN ANNUAL STATE-WIDE ANTHOLOGY
OF POETRY & PROSE BY OUR MEMBERS

A California Writers Club Original

The California Writers Club Literary Review is published annually by
The California Writers Club, a 501(c)\3 nonprofit
P.O. Box 201, Danville, CA 94526

calwriters.org

✳

ISBN 978-1-7356372-0-4

Library of Congress Cataloging-in Publication Data
California Writers Club Annual Literary Review 2020 – An annual
statewide anthology of prose & poetry by our members

1. American poetry – 21st century
2. American short prose – 21st century
I.   Title: California Writers Club Annual Literary Review 2020
II. California Writers Club

*Book design & production by Fred Dodsworth
Contact: fdodsworth@comcast.net*

*Front cover photograph: Talavera, by Monique Richardson, Tri Valley
Back cover photograph, Wood Bridge, by Shawn Langwell, Redwood*

Printed by BR Printing in San Jose, California

THE CALIFORNIA WRITERS CLUB, a 501(c)3 educational nonprofit corporation, was founded in 1909 out of the lively literary scene in San Francisco's East Bay region that flourished in the first decade of the 20th century. The CWC was incorporated in 1913 and has held meetings for over 100 years. Today the CWC has more than 2000 members in 22 branches throughout the state, and remains one of the oldest organizations for writers in continuous operation in the nation.

CWC's mission is to educate members and the public in the craft and business of writing and opens membership to writers of all interests, levels, and genres. Our website, *calwriters.org*, has specific information about membership and links to the individual branches.

BRANCHES & (MEETING LOCATIONS)

Berkeley (Berkeley/Oakland)
cwc-berkeley.org

Central Coast (Pacific Grove)
centralcoastwriters.org

Central Dunes (Nipomo)
coastaldunescwc.com

East Sierra (Ridgecrest)
ridgewriters.wordpress.com

Fremont (Fremont)
cwc-fremontareawriters.org

High Desert (Apple Valley)
hdcwc.com

Inland Empire (Ontario)
iecwc.com

Long Beach (Long Beach)
calwriterslongbeach.org

Marin (Corte Madera)
cwcmarin.com

Mendocino (Mendocino)
writersmendocinocoast.org

Mt. Diablo (Pleasant Hill)
cwcmtdiablo.org

Napa Valley (Napa)
napavalleywriters.net

North State (Chico)
northstatewriters.com

Orange County (Orange)
calwritersorangecounty.org

Redwood (Santa Rosa)
redwoodwriters.org

Sacramento (Rancho Cordova)
cwcsacramentowriters.org

San Fernando Valley (Woodland Hills)
cwc-sfv.org

San Joaquin Valley (Stockton)
sanjoaquinvalleywriters.org

SF/Peninsula (Redwood City)
cwc-peninsula.org

South Bay (San Jose)
southbaywriters.com

Tri-Valley (Pleasanton)
trivalleywriters.org

Writers of Kern (Bakersfield)
writersofkern.com

Publishing Team

EDITOR
FRED DODSWORTH, *Berkeley*
ACQUISITION EDITORS
JEANETTE FRATTO, *Orange County*
RENEE GEFFKEN, *Coastal Dunes*
DAVE LaROCHE, *South Bay*
JANA McBURNEY-LIN, *South Bay*
MARK SCOTT PIPER, *Redwood*
EVA POOLE-GILSON, *East Sierra*
COLLEEN RAE, *Marin*
JACQUELINE MUTZ, *South Bay*
DOROTHY RICE, *Sacramento*
ALINE SOULES, *Mt. Diablo*
ANDREW SOUND, *East Sierra*
PAM TALLMAN, *Orange County*
ELISABETH TUCK, *Mt. Diablo*
ASSUNTA MARIA VICKERS, *Inland Empire*
PROOFREADERS
ROGER LUBECK, *Redwood*
KYMBERLIE INGALLS, *Napa Valley*

INTAKE MANAGER
DAVID GEORGE, *Mt. Diablo*
TRAFFIC MANAGER
LINDA SAHOLT, *East Sierra*
ART DIRECTION/PRODUCTION
FRED DODSWORTH, *Berkeley*

PRINTING/MAILING: BR PRINTING, SAN JOSE, CA

✳

CWC Officers

PRESIDENT DONNA McCROHAN ROSENTHAL, *East Sierra*
VICE PRESIDENT ROGER LUBECK, *Redwood Writers*
TREASURER ANTHONY BECKER, *Inland Empire*
SECRETARY ELISABETH TUCK, *Mt. Diablo*

TABLE OF CONTENTS

✳

COVID-19: SUDDENLY IT ALL CHANGED

The year 2020 began with excellent projects and programs in place for our 22 branches. Then Covid-19 struck. While face-to-face gatherings couldn't continue, branches rose to the challenge. Many offered virtual meetings, inventive contests, and one-of-a-kind publishing opportunities to fully engage our creative community. A new excellence emerged. We discovered untapped resources we didn't know we had.

On the state level, we received over 300 submissions for *The 2020 Literary Review*, revealing more excellence from every corner of realm. Our talented, dedicated, and patient editorial team combed through the bounty, making difficult decisions to select the very best. We congratulate the writers whose work we showcase in these pages. As a timely bonus, we've added an excerpt from Jack London's (1876-1916) science fiction classic *The Scarlet Plague* (opposite page). Ever the adventurer Jack London returns to our pages in the story of legendary surfer George Freeth story beginning on page 58.

We've come a long way since South Bay's David LaRoche launched our first *Literary Review* in 2012. It matured and flourished thanks to his vision and perseverance. Today it represents two important, tangible benefits: members receive *The Literary Review* free, and only members may submit for publication.

Twelve years later, you'll find love, loss, laughter, betrayal, healing, heroism, redwoods, a dragon and more in this edition. Read. Enjoy. Start drafting, crafting, and polishing your submission(s) for *The 2021 Literary Review*.

If you haven't paid your dues yet, please don't delay. Whatever has changed, we're still here and we will continue to serve your needs as a writer, and we will meet again. Sail on!

Donna McCrohan Rosenthal
CWC President

The Scarlet Plague

(an excerpt)

"It slew so swiftly when once it manifested itself, that we were led to believe that the period of incubation was equally swift. So, when two days had left us unscathed, we were elated with the idea that we were free of the contagion. But the third day disillusioned us"

...

"To think of it! I've seen this beach alive with men, women, and children on a pleasant Sunday. And there weren't any bears to at them up, either. And right up on the cliff was a big restaurant where you could get anything you wanted to eat. Four million people lived in San Francisco then. And now in the whole city and county there aren't forty all told."

...

"Where four million people disported themselves, the wild wolves roam to-day, and the savage progeny of our loins, with prehistoric weapons, defend themselves against the fanged despoilers. Think of it! And all because of the Scarlet Death –"

✳

In the early 1900s, San Francisco's Bay Area literary notables included Jack London, Ina Coolbrith, George Sterling, and Joaquin Miller. Their casual gatherings led to the beginnings of what became The California Writers Club *in 1909. Best known for adventure novels, London also gave us his science fiction classic* The Scarlet Plague: *Set in a post-apocalyptic 2073, sixty years after a pandemic, it strikes too close to home in 2020.*

originally published in London Magazine *in 1912*

WE **ATTENDED A POLISH-MEXICAN WEDDING** which first appeared as an unharmonious gathering of cultures but gradually blended together into a jovial celebration. A party that featured kielbasa sausages and enchiladas coexisting at the buffet table along with an accordion player who could play both polkas and Norteña style. When the piercing blare from the mariachi horn players relented for a short time and a slow jam finally played, my tipsy wife Linda grabbed my arm and off we went to the dance floor. We shuffled around like two weary prizefighters locked in a clinch.

My mind drifted off to a previous version of the same event. I was transported to my eighth-grade graduation celebration when Charlene Bowers asked me to slow dance. She so towered over me that it took four years for me to catch up to her in height. When the song ended, she tried to plant a kiss on my lips which caught me off guard. The smooch didn't land on target, and we bumped heads. She reloaded and went in for some more action but this time I squared up, and we made a perfect connection. That moment in time was gone in a matter of seconds but has never left my memory decades later.

WHAT IS MARITAL BLISS?
Chris Weilert

The wedding reception checked off all the boxes on the events scorecard, the final one being the cake cutting where the newlyweds guide the slice into each other's mouth comedy act. We said our goodbyes and congratulations then made our way to the exit but not before we ran into my ex-wife, Sandy. If I had known she still kept in touch with Skip and Melanie, the groom's parents who we befriended when we were together, I wouldn't have attended. All the years of wondering what it would be like if we ever met each other again but to have my two wives in the same place at the same time was never part of that thought process. Time stopped followed by double takes to make sure we were seeing things right. She still dyed her hair dark brown and applied a gob of red lipstick.

Both wives appeared to be unembarrassed by this situation unlike me who wanted the meeting to come to a swift resolution. "Sandy, meet Linda, Linda meet Sandy" is all I managed to say before control of the conversation was taken away from me. After the introduction, I envisioned all of this unfolding where my carcass was going to be picked clean. I know the wheels in their heads were turning while sweat rolled down my back.

After a little small talk, I grabbed Linda's arm,

"We should go, it's getting late and I have a huge day tomorrow...of chores and I need to go to Home Depot to buy some wood."

I placed my hand on her shoulder and immediately she stiffened up like she wasn't going anywhere. No words came out of my mouth, and they both laughed at my expense. They knew they had me in a tight spot, and both wanted the torture to continue.

Sandy did the unthinkable, she declared, "We should get a drink." I held my composure and declined the invitation before Linda could respond. No such luck, Linda declared, "It would be okay if we stayed a little longer" and guided us to the bar. The walk of death. I dreaded a future where they are now friends. The chance, the odds and why in the hell did this have to happen clouded my mind.

"So, Sandy, where do you live?" Linda asked.

"Not too far from you two, I'm over in Placerville."

"Oh, nice... we pass through all the time."

"Well, you should stop in and say hello, or we can go for lunch in downtown," Sandy replied.

At this point I am not being included in their conversation. I stared out at the wedding party and pitied the groom because he looked exhausted. All he probably wanted to do was get back to his bedroom and pass out. Meanwhile, these two interviewed each other, my wife acted like a realtor.

Every man can't help contemplating how one rates with the women of his past and present. You just hope they all remember the great moments and contract amnesia of the not so.

"We checked out homes in the area and found they are still quite reasonably priced."

"You know what? There is a cute three-bedroom two-bath on my street that just went up on the market," Sandy said with her brown eyes wide open along with her smile, still crooked as ever.

The next twenty minutes lasted longer than my first marriage. Fortunately, I wasn't the subject of the conversation, but more about the two of them and their newfound BFF status. Every man can't help contemplating how one rates with the women of his past and present. You just hope they all remember the great moments and contract amnesia of the not so. This would be wishful thinking. In my opinion, they seem to recall every shortfall you ever displayed even if it happened only once.

On the way home, I brought this theory up to my wife, and she replied,

"Those shortfalls would need to be fairly awful for us to remember, like the time you didn't stick up for me when I got into a huge shouting match with Brenda, our old neighbor about feeding birds in our backyard."

"We've been over that a million times, bird poop was all over her yard and I felt sorry for her," I said and rolled my eyes.

I called a truce before we started down this path again. Instead, Linda went on to tell me she really wanted to understand why the marriage didn't last without outright questioning my ex. I asked her if she got it all resolved in her mind in the brief amount of time. She pondered for a couple of seconds then retorted, "Well, I am not very sure but obviously she was way too short for you."

South Bay

Bear, photo by Allene Symons, Long Beach

SIMONA CARINI

End of Summer in Northern California

To those

who say our state

has no real fall: Notice

how warmer light paints cliffs ocher

after noon. Walk on roads where pink naked

ladies bloom. Run in Redwood Park and watch deer hop

among ferns turned brown. Hike Sierra trails strewn with golden

leaves showered by quaking aspen. At dawn, crack the frozen

stream near your tent. Fog no longer rolls in at day's

end, chilling you. See the horizon at

sunrise draw a sharp line between

ocean and sky. Hear trees

exhale in our

first rain.

Redwood Writers

ONE *OF THE PERKS OF BEING A STAFF MEMBER* at the university is a reduced membership to the campus' weight room facilities—with access to the gym limited to staff and faculty only (no students) from noon to 2:00 p.m.

I signed up, knowing I wouldn't be surrounded by young hardbodies to make me feel old and frumpy or roll their eyes when I bared my everything in the locker room. I couldn't wait to start a workout routine, and when my bum tightened and an inch disappeared off my waistline, I turned into a fanatic.

One morning, in my rush to get dressed for work, I stuffed what gym attire I needed into my Adidas bag, then cursed myself when I remembered my sports bra was still in the washing machine. I'm petite and not big busted, so I decided my having to go braless under my gym tee wasn't a big deal. I zipped my bag shut, grabbed my purse, and headed for the office.

PEEK-A-BOO
Kathi Hiatt

When noontime rolled around, I made my way across campus to the women's locker room, and from there to the weight room. As is the case with most fitness centers, all attempts to conceal rude noises are left at the door; bodybuilding and powerlifting exercises come with an unwritten promise to extract loud testosterone (and estrogen) grunts and a variety of other obscene (and sometimes smelly) noises. I took a moment to watch as sweat-stained staff and faculty members (mostly male) strained to push, pull, and lift more weight than they should. Because weight and bodybuilding are considered individual sports, checking out the competition is done discreetly.

I peeled off my new Nike jacket (a trendy fashion statement is important) and decided to begin my workout with one of the torture machines designed to strengthen back muscles and triceps. The horizontal bar hovering just above my head connected to pulleys and cables that hooked up to a stack of five-pound bars. The machine's design allowed the user to increase or decrease the five-pound weights by simply removing and reinserting a steel pin into the bars. I was feeling frisky, so I added two more bars to my routine. I scanned the gym, hoping someone would notice and be impressed. No one was.

After assuming the proper stance under the horizontal bar (legs apart, feet forward), I pulled the bar with the added ten pounds of weight down to my waist. "Whoa," I wheezed, "heavier than I thought." I let the cabled pulleys slowly pull the bar back up to its starting position. Not wanting anyone else in the gym to know I had added too much weight, I pulled the hanging bar down to my waist a second time. "Whoa," I wheezed again, loosening my grip and letting the bar slide back up. "Really freak'n heavy."

Still not willing to admit that I had over-extended myself, I pulled the bar down to my waist a third time. Before I had a chance to loosen my grip and allow the bar to return once again to its starting position, the cable tie connecting the horizontal bar snagged a small hole in the bottom of my tee-shirt and began pulling it up. I tried to bring the bar back down so I could unhook the snagged tee, but the burning pain in my triceps had placed a toll on my stamina; the horizontal bar continued its upward crawl—pulling the bottom of my tee-shirt towards my chin. In a panic, I sucked in a deep breath, and with a deep guttural grunt that Arnold Schwarzenegger would have been proud of, I tried again to force the bar back down—to no avail. My muscle strength was exhausted. When I felt the cold sting of the airconditioned room on my exposed stomach, my fight to pull the bar back down turned into panic. My adrenaline rose to record levels. Sweat poured down the sides of my beet-red face; my heart pounded against the inside my chest; little by little, I was losing the battle. When the cold steel of the horizontal bar pressed against my bottom lip, panic fizzled to hopelessness. I stood on tippy-toes and peered in wide-eyed horror over the top of the still-rising bar. "Help me," I rasped.

Upon seeing my dilemma, the university registrar hurried to my rescue from the opposite side of the gym. All eyes in the room fixated on me and the sprinting registrar, who jerked the bar back down to my waist and freed the snagged tee. I yanked the shirt over my exposed midriff, noted the enlarged hole along the hemline, and looked around at my colleagues. The stunned silence and failed attempts to smother smiles convinced me the registrar had been unsuccessful in his attempt to save me from humiliation.

For the next several months, I ate my lunch at my desk and refused to go anywhere near the physical education building. After a ten-pound weight gain gave me the courage I needed to restart my workouts, I reluctantly made my way back to the women's locker room.

Maybe the constrained smiles of my colleagues had been imagined. I told myself as I trudged toward the gym. *Maybe I hadn't actually flashed everyone. My friends always accuse me of turning every situation into a worst-case scenario.* The closer I got to the gym, the more convinced I became my dignity was saved by the registrar—just in the nick of time. The unpleasant memories of the whole ordeal began to diminish—a warm sense of relief washed over me. For the first time in months, I was no longer dreading the smirks I feared I would face when I re-entered the weight room. I sat my gym bag down and popped open my locker—all doubt as to whether I had flashed the entire gym was removed. Dangling from a clothes hook were several long strands of colorful glass beads, much like those the chest-baring coeds earn during Mardi Gras.

North State Writers

Flower, photo by Audrey Kalman, SF/Peninsula.

ALAN TRAXLER LIVES IN TWO HOMES. He owns a home with his parents in the mountain village of Magalia. He also is an assistant manager at a residential home for four men with special needs called Redwood House in Paradise, California. Thirty years old, this gentle bear of a man has a smile and a high-five for everyone. When he walks through the door of Redwood House, everyone calms down. They are his second family. He takes them for van rides when one of them is upset or agitated. They go to the Wild Cat games at Chico State and camp on the Mendocino coast. Sometimes they just hang out at Bille Park or the duck pond.

REDWOOD TRIBUTE
Joan Goodreau

On November 8, 2018, Alan wakes up relaxed in his Magalia home. No doctor's appointment to take his dad to. No shopping at Grocery Outlet. Just an easy day off to chill and hang out with his adopted calico cat, Sweetness. Maybe watch a Falcons game and pick up some Papa Murphy's pizzas for the family. The only decisions he needs to make today is what pizza topping to get. Taylor, his sister, likes plain cheese, but his favorite is sausage.

Then his cell phone rings and Willie Davidson, the manager at Redwood House, tells him of the fire. Flames lick and devour ancient pines and redwoods. Schools, stores, restaurants erupt and explode. The fire roars like thunder. Paradise is an inferno. The sixty staff and residents in the seventeen homes of California Vocations residential and supported living homes pack up. There is no time to gather and save. Just grab and go and hope to make it down the ridge alive.

They leave their homes behind to the fire which roars, spits spark,, and cremates beds, photo albums and Giant's jerseys. In vans they creep down Skyway Drive, bumper to bumper, with flames jumping and smoke black as midnight.

Alan drives down the back way from Magalia to look for the escaped caravan. The ridge above is a crack of red blood like an open wound. Finally, he finds them at the Three Bridges RV Camp in the grey haze of smoke and cinders beside the Sacramento River.

The four guys from their incinerated Redwood House don't sleep much that night. They stay with all the others at the Community Building in the camp. They look for their beds but cannot find them. Pace, cry, shriek through the night into another day. The smoke eclipses the sun when it rises, and the eerie light like dusk lasts all day.

> Lives eclipsed by smoke
> search by the river churning
> for what is lost.

But Alan does not disappear in the fire. He believes presence is everything. There he is—steady and calm, no matter what is going on around him This is nothing new for Alan. Ever since he was young, he always looked out for his sister and cousins. They would go hiking and he would walk behind to be the last one to make sure everyone kept together and stayed safe. From the beginning, he was a shepherd to watch out and care for others. Redwood House moves from the RV Camp to a motel room in Corning for a few days until they can find space at a Mental Health Unit at Yuba City. Here at this lock-down unit, the guys smell the musty air and feel the old walls close in on them. They remember from years past before they came to California Vocations. How they were trapped by take-downs and no escape. But Alan is with them now, and he wears his calm like a cloak and spreads it over the old, broken-down residence to cover everyone. In less than a month, they live in a camp, a hotel room, a mental health lock-down facility.

> Belonging nowhere
> their home, safe space is Alan
> who's ever present.

Willie tells Alan to take some time off to rest and try to get rid of a lingering cold and cough made worse by the smoke. He does not take much time off because one-third of the staff quit. Their homes are gone and they leave to live with family and friends. His house in Magalia does not burn down, but it is damaged and his mom, dad and sister are living in a motel.

The remaining staff work long days, sixty hours a week or more. Alan stays where he is needed. Finally, by Thanksgiving, Redwood house and the other homes move to the Migrant Farm Labor Housing in Williams, California. The staff as well as the men and women with special needs live side-by-side in small apartment units (barracks).

He takes on consecutive day and night shifts. His manager, Willie, thinks of Alan as the rock everyone depends on. When there is trouble among the roommates, Alan knows how to fix it. Soft-spoken, known as the gentle giant with a big heart, he talks people down from their crises.

He stays with his guys through the cold, the rain, and his lingering chest cold. When one of them comes down with pneumonia, he stays with him in the hospital to make sure he is not afraid. Alan didn't identify with his favorite Marvel heroes, but he was Iron Man to the men at Redwood.

He helps with the Christmas festivities to give their Williams community and its band of uprooted exiles the holiday spirit. Santa finds them all in Williams and rides in on a fire truck with loads of gifts. After all that excitement, the men at Redwood finally go to sleep. Another late night and early morning for Willie and Alan. They drink a beer in their shared apartment.

"You know, it's difficult now," says Alan. "But we'll look back on this time and see it differently than we see it now. In the future, we'll miss these days and the fun we had together. Here's to the future. Here's to Redwood," says Alan and they clink bottles to a better time to come. Willie grins and realizes that Alan is the first to look into the future and see how they had lived through this hard time as a community.

In the New Year, Alan finally decides to follow Willie's advice and take some time off. His house had been repaired from the fire damage, and his family had returned. He plans to take his father for his doctor's check-up, maybe play Destiny Video Game or Connect Four, or just catch up with his sister. Maybe even go to Outpatient Care about his cough that got worse in the cold, wet air of Williams.

He looks forward to going home to Magalia. The house still needs work, but it did not burn down and they can live in it as a family again. He is tired from the hour-and-a-half drive from Williams or maybe all those extra shifts, so he goes to bed early.

The next morning his parents let him sleep in late. They know how hard he has worked. But breakfast is getting cold, so his mother goes to his room to wake him. But he does not wake. Death has come from undiagnosed bronchial pneumonia and a heart condition.

The day of the funeral is a bright, sunny day. But inside Our Divine Savior Catholic Church, it is dark and the shroud of shock covers the family. Alan's many friends look around almost expecting him to suddenly appear. "Where's Alan? We can always depend on him to be here when we need him." Flames from the candles on the altar give a small light in the darkness. Bob Irvine, head of California Vocations, says, "Alan Traxler was a gift to everyone he touched. He'll be missed every day, but he will never be forgotten."

In the spring, the men at Redwood House move back to Butte County into permanent housing, and Alan's presence goes with them. From the ashes and smoke, they carry the memory of him. Presence is everything.

> He the redwood stands
> rooted in memory to
> guard and guide us on.

On days off would help his family.
Knew what was wrong before they knew it. Could walk into the home and the place would calm down, including the staff. He knew what to do.
He would take them on rides in the van when they were restless or upset.
He wore his calm like a cloak and spread it out over the home to protect it.
After the fire, Redwood was gone, but their home survived. Alan was their home.

His cold and cough got worse, but he did not bother with doctors.
Friendly giant. Bear.

We will remember these times. They have been hard.
Competitive in games.

North State Writers

Yuma Cemetary photo by Carol Kearns, Long Beach.

MY FATHER **DID NOT DIE** of aspiration pneumonia. That's what his death certificate states, but it's not true. They wouldn't allow me to write in the real reason. A death certificate requires a cause of death. A person isn't permitted to just die. There must be something to blame, something that goes wrong as if death is a mistake. But death happens to everyone. My dad knew that. That's why he planned his one-hundredth birthday as a memorial service for himself.

✶✶✶

December third, 2018 was his one-hundredth birthday. What a celebration it was! A week full of festivities. Hiking a mile in the redwoods with his Swedish cousins. Going to San Francisco and picking up the children of life-long friends and then taking them around Golden Gate Park. A five-course French dinner for 21 people. And then on his actual birthday a celebration in the style of a Unitarian Universalist memorial service.

EVERYONE DOES IT
Jan Ögren

My dad stood behind the podium, in his pink dress shirt and bolo tie, at the beginning of his 100th birthday celebration, looking out at the crowd of 130 people and said, "This is my memorial service, and I am here! Too often I've been at memorial services and the person being honored isn't there. That doesn't seem right. So I'm here for mine." He smiled and looked around as people cheered him. He raised his arms high above his head, clasping his hands as though he'd just won a gold medal.

"Thank you for coming. To light the chalice for my service, I'm going to read a poem called 'Choose Life.' Three years ago my daughter told me she wanted to dedicate her next book to me, and what would I like? Right away I said I want a book of your poetry and photography. I got to pick out all my favorite poems and this one is the title poem from the book *Choose Life.*"

He read the poem, as I lit the chalice. Then my dad continued, "People ask me how did I do it? How is that I'm one hundred years old and happy? Well, I'm going to tell you my five philosophies." He reached up and tapped his forehead. "Think positively. Try something new. Look forward to growing older. Yes, I did say look forward to growing older! Work to build a better world for all. And exercise daily, or almost daily." He added the last with a smile. Even though he did exercise every day, he didn't want to discourage anyone if they didn't do it daily.

The minister said it was the most joyful memorial service he'd ever performed. It was also the easiest because my dad wrote out the script for him; after all, he did like to be in control. The minister shared how my father was raised Swedish Methodist on a small farm in Minnesota. He left that faith when he went to the University of Minnesota. It was too confining for him, just like living on a farm was not the life he wanted. He was an explorer. He wanted to figure out life for himself, not be told what to believe or what to do every day.

When my dad discovered Unitarian Universalism he knew he'd found a spiritual home. Here was a religion that allowed him to be an atheist, and later an agnostic. He lived without a belief or a concept of what would happen after death and for him, it was the big unknown.

We showed pictures of him, we sang songs and people got up and talked about him, just like they'd do at a memorial service. Only he got to be there for all of it. At the end my dad came back up to do the closing words. "I started my service with the poem 'Choose Life,'" he said. "Now I'm going to end with two poems about death. The first one is called. 'I Plan to Die.' I've always been annoyed when people say 'if I die' as though it's an option. It's not. Everyone will die. The second poem is called, 'Pack Love' about how all you need for your last journey is love." He read the two poems and then everyone sang happy birthday to him. The pianist, who was a professional jazz musician, played a boogie-woogie improve on happy birthday and my dad and I danced on stage, as the audience sprang to their feet and cheered him.

✳✳✳

Eighteen days after his birthday Dad decided to go on hospice. He didn't want someone calling an ambulance and sending him to the hospital, as he got ready to die. There was an obstacle to his qualifying for hospice though, he had no terminal diagnosis. He was in good health. But since he was 100 years old the nurse said, "We'll admit you, then reevaluate you in three months."

After filling out all the paperwork he turned to me and asked, "Do we still have time to go to that Irish Christmas show tonight?"

"Sure, Dad," I said, "why not go out and celebrate going on hospice." It was a good way to avoid thinking that he was planning to die. The poem he read at his memorial, 'I Plan to Die,' begins: "I plan to die. Not next Thursday and not before the holidays." And he did that. He lived through Christmas and New Year's so that he wouldn't leave us with his death over the holidays. The poem ends with the line: "All my life, I have planned, as my final act - to die." And that's what he did on January fifth, two weeks after entering hospice.

I wish I'd asked him more about how he knew he was going to die. Every time I tried, I got so choked up with tears it was hard to talk, and then we'd just look at each other and we knew. We knew the time was coming and he wanted to die naturally, in good health.

He didn't die of any cause or reason. He died because he knew how to let go. He'd been practicing it for years. Letting go of friends, letting go of his much-beloved wife, letting go of being able to travel long distances, letting go of being able to cross-country ski and climb mountains.

People asked me if there would be a memorial service, but I said, "No, we had it, he planned it, and he was there." We did have a brief service with the minister and forty people when we put his ashes in the memorial garden at the church. My mother died in 2013, just after their sixty-fourth anniversary. Her ashes were placed in the memorial garden and every time I took my dad to church, we paused at the garden. He would point to where her ashes were and say, "someday that's where I'll be, right next to her."

His final words, that the minister read were, "I enjoy life. Each step along the way has given me new experiences. I don't look back at the past with regrets or nostalgia. Every year has been the best yet."

Redwood Writers

Trinity Library photo by Jill Hedgecock, Mt Diablo

SOMETIMES *A FAMILY SECRET* is so well hidden, you didn't know it was there, but once uncovered it fills in the blanks of a fractured story. Usually, it's after the person died so you can't ask about it. You're left making stuff up. And so, I begin piecing together the tale of my Aunt Charlotte.

My memories of her are sensory. The smell of her kitchen, the earthiness of her garden, and the light in her bay window full of African violets. As a young child, I wasn't sure where Africa was in relation to New Jersey; I just knew the violets bloomed year-round, even in the snowy winter. She told me the light in the window carried magic. I used to wish I could crawl into that window, soak up the magic, and fly away—usually to Africa.

In the summer, her garden was overgrown with cucumbers, radishes, and carrots. None of which appealed to my young taste buds. But the sunflowers! They were my secret hiding place. When I heard the story of the garden of Eden in catechism class, I thought of Aunt Charlotte's backyard. The smell of freshly turned dirt and bits of lavender would cling to me as I came in for dinner. Her kitchen, unlike my mother's, was in constant creation of something sweet. She embraced the concept of dessert the way she embraced me when I ran up the porch steps and into her strong and loving arms.

CAUGHT IN THE VENUS FLYTRAP
Korie Pelka

I was nine when my family moved to Arizona and my relationship with Aunt Charlotte grew distant. It wasn't until I graduated from eighth grade that I had the opportunity to visit her on my own. Now, through the eyes of a fourteen-year-old young woman, I had new insights.

I'd finally done the math and figured out my cousin was the reason she had to marry my uncle. She'd gotten pregnant and was forced into marriage to save her reputation. No one in my family ever acknowledged or discussed it.

So, I entered our conversations during my visit with a sense of curiosity, wondering if there were other secrets that might allow me to glimpse the woman behind the role of "aunt." As we sat around the kitchen table, shucking peas and rolling pie crust, she treated me as an adult. It was a new experience and I reveled in it. It was obvious she needed to talk, and I was an eager listener.

What I heard, although she never admitted it, was that she was in love with another man—and had been since high school. His name was Emmett and they were still friends. In fact, for almost two decades, they'd gone camping together several times a year; she with her husband and Emmett with his friend Carl. Yes, his friend Carl. I knew a gay relationship when I heard it. Yet after all these years, she was still in love with him. From what I heard, he loved her too. Just not in the way she wanted and needed. My heart ached for her when I saw her light up talking about Emmett and how quickly that light died when her husband came home.

Watching her reminded me of catching fireflies in her back yard when I was five. I usually set them free . . . except for this particular night.

Charlotte had a Venus flytrap - yet another misplaced, exotic plant in the suburbs of Jersey. I didn't believe it could capture flies and eat them. My logical little mind needed proof. Absent any willing house flies, Charlotte took one of my fireflies and fed it to the Venus flytrap. Sure enough, it closed up while I watched in childlike fascination as the light blinked slower and slower. I cried to let it out, but the damage was done.

What I heard, although she never admitted it, was she was in love with another man —and had been since high school.

The lesson from that night—the one that taught me how hard it is to break away once a force of nature has taken hold of you—that lesson came rushing back when Charlotte died suddenly at age fifty-four.

The autopsy revealed she died of cirrhosis of the liver. The woman who had dreams of Africa in her bay window and images of Eden in her garden, that woman also drank. Silently, every day, for decades.

The entire family was stunned.

At the time, I didn't understand how we missed the signs.

Now, I've come to see this as another version of "don't ask, don't tell." Don't ask if she's been drinking, she might tell you yes. With that comes a responsibility to help her. Don't ask if her heart is breaking when her son comes home from Vietnam, broken in spirit and deep into drugs. She might say yes, and you'd have to sit with her through the pain. Don't ask if her heart belongs to an enchanting gay man while trapped in an awful, loveless marriage. She might say yes, and you'd have to help her break free.

To my knowledge, no one ever asked those questions.

Her secret, so well kept, like her bouffant hairdo and exquisite china closet, her secret was entwined in a web of intoxication.

After the funeral, we found fifths of gin hidden throughout the house—in the overhead ceiling light, under the bed in the spare room, behind the mixer in the kitchen cabinet. We even found a bottle or two in the garden shed. You couldn't go more than eight feet from one bottle to the next, a well-planned safety net, a web invisible to everyone but Charlotte.

They asked me if I wanted any of her things, mementos to remember her by. I wandered through the house, knowing I couldn't bottle the smells of her kitchen or the warmth of her smile. All I really wanted were her African violets and that damn Venus flytrap.

SF/Peninsula

Abandoned photo by Monica A. Kuhlmann, High Desert.

I **MET MARCUS** in a web design class at the local community college. His first words to me, on the initial day of class, raised my social barriers. As I waited by the locked door to the classroom—ten minutes early for the scheduled start time—I heard a young male voice behind me say, "Hey, grandma-type lady? You takin' this class?"

I turned around to see a very thin, very oddly dressed young man standing behind me. He had shoulder-length dreadlocks partially covered by one of the scruffiest knit hats I'd ever seen. His T-shirt was emblazoned with a skull and crossbones and text of some kind in an extremely intricate font that I couldn't begin to read. His jeans were threadbare and torn in multiple places, and on his feet were glaringly bright, orange high-top tennies, no ties. But it was his face that put me off the most. He had the most alarming array of safety pins decorating—can I honestly use "decorating" for such an unpleasant sight?—every possible place on his face: several through each eyebrow, three through one nostril, two through the other, and one at each corner of his mouth. Knowing all too well the habits of current teenagers, I was fairly certain the safety pin accessorizing continued on to his ears, although the abundance of hair precluded my actually confirming that suspicion.

GRANDMA-TYPE LADY AND SAFETY-PIN FACE
Jenny Margotta

"Yes, I'm taking Mr. Wallace's Flash class." Turning back around, I hoped my cool tone of voice and obvious reluctance to continue the conversation would send him on his way. Not so.

"Cool, grandma-type lady. How come you're back in college?"

Would this offensive person ever leave me alone? If this was the caliber of students at the college, I was beginning to be sorry I'd signed up for the class. But I'd long ago been taught it was rude to ignore a direct question, so I turned once again to speak with my tormentor. I wasn't about to tell him the real reason, but I thought quickly and gave him what I hoped would be a believable answer. "I've grown bored with my life and just want to expand my knowledge, that's all."

"More power to ya', then. That's rad." The silver stud through the middle of his tongue flashed in the overhead lights.

What was this kid? Some kind of hippy throwback wannabe? Did young people really still talk like that? My personal musings were cut short by the arrival of a well-dressed gentleman. He was impeccably garbed in crisp, pressed sports pants, a tweed coat with leather patches on the elbows, and a pipe sticking out of his breast pocket. Not a strand of his pure white hair was out of place. The epitome of a college professor—and the exact opposite of my odious companion. There was no doubt in my mind that this latest arrival was none other than our instructor, Mr. Wallace. He proceeded to open the classroom door, turn on the lights, and move to the front of the room. Good, I thought, here's the instructor. I can now get away from this deplorable young man.

It was not to be. For some reason, Safety-pin Face had decided I was his long-lost grandparent or newest best friend. As I took my seat, he slid into the one next to me. Cracking his chewing gum and ceaselessly jiggling his foot up and down, his jittery, never-still antics soon began to annoy me even more than his seeming inability to shut up. For the next five minutes, I was treated to a non-stop monologue of his life's history, not that I bothered to listen.

Finally, Mr. Wallace called the class to order and began taking roll. About halfway through the approximately thirty people in the room, he called out, "Marcus Symes?"

"Yo," my seating companion replied.

You can imagine my surprise when Mr. Wallace paused in his roll call. "Marcus, I'm so glad to see you're taking one of my classes again. I've missed you the last few semesters."

Marcus, my perforated-faced shadow, laughed and replied, "Missed you, too, teach. You up to date on all your material, or you gonna want my help again?"

Oh, nice, I thought. It's bad enough he's latched on to me in a totally unacceptable manner. I'm just another student. But to lack the manners to treat the teacher respectfully, well ... that's just not right. I shot a look of reproach at Marcus. He either failed to see it or chose to ignore it.

Once roll call ended and class began, however, an unbelievable change came over the twitching, jiggling, irreverent young man. He immediately stopped talking, pulled a laptop computer from his backpack and, for the next ninety minutes, hung on every word the instructor uttered. And asked several very intelligent questions, I might add. By the end of that first session, I realized there was much more to this unattractive teenager than I first gave him credit for.

At the end of the class, he turned to me once again. "Hey, grandma-type lady. You got a name? Mine's Marcus. See ya on Thursday." Not waiting for my reply, he jumped up and skipped—yes, actually skipped—out of the room.

Over the course of the next six weeks, my initial opinion of Marcus did a complete 180. I was in awe of his grasp of computers, software, internet technology, electronics—there didn't seem to be anything about those areas Marcus didn't know. He could have taught the class we were taking, so extensive was his knowledge. I even asked him at one point why he was taking the class. He just smiled and said, "Gotta have the creds for that sheepskin, ya know."

One evening Marcus asked me, "Grandma-type lady, you interested in gettin' a cuppa coffee with me after class? A Coke or somethin', maybe?" I'd long since told Marcus to call me Tabitha, but he insisted on his own style of formality. "Oh, I could never call an older woman by her first name," was his reply. "Guy's gotta have some manners."

Unknown to Marcus, I was eager to meet with him away from class. A plan had been forming in my mind for some time, and I had a sneaking suspicion that Marcus was just the person to help me with it.

Perhaps this is the time for a little background on me. I was indeed old enough to be a grandmother—having just turned sixty a few months previously—although I was not, in fact, a grandmother. I had no children at all, truth be told. I did have a brother and a sister but had been estranged from them for nearly thirty years. It's a long story, much too complicated to go into here. Besides, those relationships were not germane to my immediate problem. My immediate problem was my husband, Dale Henry Mahoney. Dale Henry, you see, was addicted to gambling.

At the time of this writing, Dale Henry owed, as near as I knew, a little over $92,000 in gambling debts. Our credit cards had all been maxed out, we were three months behind on the mortgage, he'd pawned everything of value he could get his hands on, and he had tapped every friend and acquaintance he could think of for loans. The constant phone calls for collection attempts were growing increasingly threatening. Add to that the fact that Dale Henry had decided the best way to alleviate his stress was to use me as his personal punching bag, and you can begin to understand my problems.

Over the past few months, a daring plan had come to me. I decided I was going to run away from home. Literally disappear into the world where no one could find me. *How* I was going to disappear was the problem. I had liquidated my one remaining asset that I'd carefully hidden from Dale Henry—a $100,000 life insurance policy, face value $12,153.47. Not much to start a new life on, but it would have to do. But just how does a person go about disappearing? Without creditors tracking them down?

Just the evening before, however, I'd chanced to see a program on television about computer hackers and all the databases they could hack into. The program went into some detail about how, in this electronics-based world, it was possible, with the right knowledge, to totally erase your digital existence. I had a hunch Marcus just might be able to help me with that.

"Yes, Marcus." I finally recalled where I was and realized I'd taken a long time to answer his question. "I'd like that very much." So the two of us— one of the strangest couples you've probably ever seen together—walked off to find an empty table at the nearest Starbuck's.

> *I decided I was going to run away from home. Literally disappear into the world where no one could find me.*

Once seated—me with a plain black coffee and Marcus with some $5.00-triple-latte-double-espresso-nonfat-soy-creamer-with-caramel-sauce-type concoction—I grabbed the conversation ball. After ten minutes of explanation, I took a deep breath and asked the important question. "Is that something you can do for me, Marcus? I can pay you, not much, but something."

"Grandma-type lady, don't insult me with an offer to pay. Playtime ain't pay time. And hackin's definitely my idea of playtime. 'Course I can help. Come to my place Thursday after class and we'll get you squared away." He paused, "Oh, is Thursday too soon?"

"Thursday will be fine, Marcus. Give me your address, and I'll drive straight there after class."

He laughed. "Don't have to drive. I live in the apartments above the store here. Great location. I grab their Wi-Fi signal and nobody can trace me past the shop."

Tossing the last of my coffee into the trash, I walked back to my car and made my way home. My nightly slap-around by Dale Henry didn't even faze me that night. I was going to disappear. Nothing could stop me now.

Wednesday passed in a blur. I packed and moved my bags into my neighbor's empty trash cans while Dale Henry was out of the house. My neighbors were on a month-long cruise, and the trash wasn't scheduled for pickup until the following Monday, so I knew my two small bags would go undetected until Thursday night. Thursday, I cleaned house and even made three casseroles that I wrapped in foil, neatly labeled, and stuck in the freezer. All right, so Dale Henry was an abusive sleaze; I was still his wife, and I felt duty bound to leave him with at least a few meals.

I arrived a full half hour early at the college, and the ninety-minute class seemed to last nine hours, but finally, it was over. Marcus and I walked to the Starbuck's and took the stairs up to his second-floor apartment. Expecting the apartment to reflect Marcus' lack of cleanliness and ragged appearance, I was stunned when he opened the door. The place was absolutely immaculate and crammed with racks of high-tech electronics gear. I counted a total of five laptop computers and three desktop computers, all obviously state of the art. There were enough colored lights flashing on enough pieces of equipment that I fleetingly thought that, when the lights were off, the room must look like the internal workings of a pinball machine gone wild.

"Okay, grandma-type lady," Marcus said. "Let's get started." He sat down at the largest of the laptops, cracked his knuckles several times, and started typing, his fingers flying faster than my eye could follow.

"Full name?" he snapped. "Birth date? Place of birth? Mother's full name, including maiden? Father's full name? Social security number?" One question followed the next faster than I could answer them. Each time I answered a question, I noticed a red point of light appear on the digitized map displayed on the laptop's screen. "Library card number? Checking? Savings? Credit card numbers? Mortgage?"

I dutifully answered. More questions. More lights. The screen was now crowded with them.

Finally, the questions stopped. Marcus sat silently for a time, again cracking his knuckles. His left leg was jiggling faster than ever, and I could barely restrain myself from laying a gentle, please-stop hand on his pumping kneecap. Finally, he turned towards me. "You sure you wanna do this, grandma-type lady? Once I make you disappear, you can't change your mind, ya know?"

Without hesitation, I answered, "Yes, Marcus, I'm sure."

He briefly explained that each of the little lights on the screen represented my digital presence somewhere in cyber-world. I appreciated his attempt to share his knowledge, but having come this far, I was eager to get on with it.

"Okay, then," he said when I expressed my impatience. "Watch." His fingers flew across the keyboard as he hummed a tuneless melody, his left foot again pumping non-stop. I watched the screen, fascinated, as one by one the lights began to disappear. At last there was only one little light blinking in a corner of the screen. "Last chance," he said.

"Do it, Marcus." I replied.

With a final, single keystroke, the last light winked out. The weirdest thing happened as I watched that last light disappear. It was as if twenty years of unbearable life were suddenly lifted from my shoulders. I felt young again and somehow, inexplicably free. "That's it?" I asked.

"That's it. You have now officially ceased to exist. No mortgage, no bills, no ID of any type. No husband, no family, no birth certificate, no *life*." He grinned up at me. "Now, who would you *like* to be?"

I smiled. "I've always liked the name Sarah James," I whispered.

Marcus grinned, his fingers renewed their intimate dance with the keyboard, and one by one, new little lights began to appear on his screen.

High Desert

"Le passe-Muraille," from a story by Marcel Aymé (Montmartre, Paris),
photo by Monte Swann, San Fernando Valley

THERE IS A TIME WHEN MILLIONS OF PEOPLE fall into a simultaneous trance: the type that rivals any sporting or religious event. The multitudes come from all walks of life as the lure of unfathomable wealth is at stake. The Utopia dream is evident by the number of souls pooling hard–earned money for the chance of realizing freedom, power, and wealth.

On a crisp spring evening in San Francisco, destiny is not determined by the constellation of the stars or the full moon hovering over the bay, but by numbers that have been stripped of their logical function and simplified into a random drawing of luck.

News Flash: Utopia 40 is the Largest Jackpot in America's History

★★★

Since turning thirty-eight, Leslie Harris felt a strange detachment from her life as if some main circuit in her brain had been deadened by the daily monotony. She couldn't pinpoint the cause for her general dissatisfaction. Everything was tolerable, but never wonderful.

At least today she got to join millions of other hopefuls with one Utopian 40 ticket on hand. She hustled through the city on her way home, making an impromptu visit to a Greek restaurant for takeout.

The evening was for splurging on dining and dreaming.

Dating was out of the question, since she figured she was 30 pounds away from activating a love life. With the ticket tucked in her sparse wallet, she found long overdue pleasure in entertaining immense wealth.

She got off the Muni and strolled through the Lone Mountain neighborhood to reach her flat on Fulton Street. She approached her Edwardian rental, posing like a grand lady with ornate white trim, curved windows, cloaked in slate grey and navy blue: a stately relic from the past. Four years ago, she fell into fortune when Jane Shaw, a woman in her late 80s, extended a grand and generous gesture. During the notoriously high real estate market, Jane professed she saw a good spirit in Leslie. Despite Leslie's inability to financially qualify for the place, Jane accepted half the value of what she could have received in the open market. The unspoken trade-off was a friendship with a landlord who lacked boundaries. The home was one of many that were built near former cemeteries by Jane's grandfather who accumulated tremendous wealth from the construction.

"There were thousands of bodies that had to be relocated, and tombstones were used to reinforce the ocean walls," Jane once said with a strange measure of amusement.

Leslie didn't want to think about the house's history, or the transfer of pain and hopelessness she had fought all her life. She did not believe in ghosts, but she did believe in evil—something she had buried deep in her psyche as a foster child. When Jane passed away, her grandnephew Alexander took over management of the property.

UTOPIA 40
Deanna Lutzeier

Upon Leslie's arrival home, Emma, her neighbor from the floor above, rushed down energetically holding Alexander's hand—quite a contrast to her usual melancholy state. She was a delicate and fair woman with a powerful operatic voice, which she practiced daily.

They had somehow crossed the boundaries between landlord and lover in two weeks. He nodded his head at Leslie in recognition and there was a whiff of an indescribable yet pleasing scent of musk that lingered when he passed by.

Leslie settled into the kitchen nook facing the eastern end of the Golden Gate Park. At a distance, she recognized a homeless man wearing tattered military fatigues as he wandered about, reciting a private monologue. She had seen him in the Financial District shouting "The blood- suckers are here!"

To live in an altered reality would be a scary thing, thought Leslie.

The silence was almost unbearable when it came time for the Utopia 40 drawing. Leslie nervously wrote down the numbers as they were announced live on TV. Between relishing her baklava and staring at the numbers, she imagined the grimace across her unethical boss' face if she won—she laughed whole heartedly.

In her soprano pitch, Emma shouted, "Someone won from the Financial District!" Her voice penetrated her floor and filtered down to Leslie's bottom flat.

Leslie switched to the local channel, and the news confirmed Emma's announcement. Looking at the scribbled numbers on the napkin, she pulled out her ticket. The first three numbers made her feel hopeful, the sixth excited, the ninth had her trembling in disbelief, and the last matching number caused her to forget to breathe.

What if I wrote a number incorrectly?

Leslie didn't want to confirm the numbers yet. She wanted to be prepared for either outcome. Her adrenaline kicked everything into overdrive. Her vision and hearing became sharpened as if she had awakened from a trance after the last four years. She called Tina, her best friend, and cited an emergency.

Twenty minutes later, Tina arrived with her perpetual smile. "Is everything okay? What—did your jerk of a boss lay you off?"

"No. Please sit down and let me get you a drink," said Leslie.

"Your flat—it never warms up. I don't know how you can live in a cold and dark place."

Leslie opened a bottle of cheap champagne and it bubbled over and spilled on the floor. She poured until it overflowed the glasses.

"Okay Leslie, now you're making me nervous. What's happening?"

"I might be the Utopia 40 winner."

Tina's easy demeanor vanished and a dark look swept across her face. "Wait, are you serious? How can you be unsure?"

Silence.

"You know, I have always considered you like a sister. If I won a massive fortune, I would no doubt share it with you," said Tina.

Leslie was surprised by Tina's comment, how it sounded almost insincere. They were both single women with a similar level of income, yet Leslie often found herself treating Tina. In the two seconds of silence, Tina's chest turned red and bled to her cheeks. Suddenly, the air between them grew hot.

"I will check tomorrow. I wrote the numbers haphazardly on a napkin."

"I can double check for you."

"I need to rest."

"You sure?" Tina's voice held a hint of restraint.

For the first time, Leslie felt awkward with Tina, as if they were suddenly strangers instead of friends of twenty years.

After Tina's abrupt departure, Leslie grabbed the ticket from her wallet and looked around the room for a hiding place. She recalled the Bible given to her by Sister Anne last weekend during a serendipitous stroll by The Sisters of Adoration Church. She recollected how Sister Anne said it was no accident that she came to the church, drawn in by the music, and handed her the Bible.

Leslie retrieved the Bible and opened a random page, placing the ticket there as her eyes landed on the printed Scripture.

"For the love of money is the root of all evil."

The verse startled Leslie, and she dropped the Bible to the floor; a palm leaf cross fell out of it. She picked up the book, ticket, and cross before taking a deep breath. *The next page I open may provide me an important insight.* Her unsteady hands turned to the latter half of the book, to 1 Peter 5:8.

"Discipline yourselves, keep alert. Like a roaring lion your adversary the devil prowls around, looking for someone to devour."

Something in the universe is trying to tell me something. I need to remain focused.

She pondered how the numbers materialized in her mind when she purchased the ticket. If, by great fortune she won, she would need a lawyer, a financial advisor, and probably a shrink. But first and foremost, Leslie needed to keep her head on straight.

"He is here!" cried the homeless man.

Leslie peeked outside and saw the ragged man pacing in front of the house. She called Emma, "Can you hear the man shouting outside? He has never come as close before. He is often in the Financial District warning about an invasion. Should I call the police?"

"He's crazy, Leslie. The police can't do much, they'll just move him along and then he will return with a vengeance. No worries, Alexander will ask him to leave."

After the call, Leslie stared at the same four walls that protected her from the big city. Her eyes followed the swirls of the stucco wall and the winning numbers seemed to appear among those patterns. A high pitch ringing grew in Leslie's ears as her blood pressure shot up. She plugged her fingers in her ears to stop the noise. *I should just leave. Now.* There was something about the house, the scriptures, the madman's warning, and Tina's greed that made Leslie want to run and hide.

In a matter of minutes, Emma and Alexander went out and came down the front steps.

"Stay away," cried the madman. His eyes widened but weren't focused on anything as he slowly backed away. Alexander barely stepped forward, but the man stumbled backwards, turned, and ran.

Leslie was perplexed by the madman's response. "How did Alexander make him leave? He reacted as if he saw the face of a devil."

"Alexander is a madman whisperer," laughed Emma.

Leslie felt overwhelmed; she couldn't conceive the magnitude of the wealth she might have won. It started to feel like a burden that could crush and stop her heart. Another vague and disturbing feeling emerged. *The house: it's holding me back.* She was blinded by her desire for a home and a decent life. She overlooked Jane's lack of boundaries and would pay the price. It wasn't just the home holding her back, it was her whole life:

how Tina's wrongs doubled her rights, her boss' subtle yet derogatory comments. All she needed was a good night's rest, and she'd be ready to move on, to embrace an authentic life.

"Leslie, are you okay? You seem tired. I hope you can still make my impromptu party tonight." Emma moved in closer. "I have someone for you to meet. Go inside, slip on a sexy dress, and join us for some wine. I promise, you will sleep soundly tonight." She hugged Leslie before heading back upstairs.

Leslie looked up towards Emma's flat and could see some of the guests. A man came to the window, not just any man, but a stranger who intrigued her from a distance for some time; she couldn't believe her eyes. She first caught sight of him at the Ferry Building standing alone in a corner and observing the people around him. He seemed out of place but not awkward. He was handsome in an understated way; his short, light brown hair combed nicely to the side and he wore thick rimmed glasses that made it hard to determine his age. On another occasion she spotted him, a second time, dining alone at the Wharf; he glanced over at her, and she sensed a mutual attraction between them. Her curiosity was greater than her fatigue, so she got ready.

Twenty minutes later, she entered Emma's home and found her singing along with someone at the piano. Emma loosened her ponytail and her hair fell in long and silky waves. After Emma's performance, the mystery man approached the piano and played Chopin's Nocturnes.

"Who is that man at the piano?" Leslie whispered to Alexander.

"Peter James. He's a lawyer and as you can see, a passionate pianist."

Leslie listened and studied his profile. He wasn't her usual type, yet there was something appealing about the man. The thought of the winning ticket floated like a balloon in the back of her mind as his music was like a soothing vapor in the air. She couldn't resist inhaling and allowing it to penetrate the cautious chamber of her heart.

After Emma's brief introduction and an hour of conversation, Peter and Leslie were hitting it off. Their seats faced one another and when he spoke, he leaned in close while his knee touched her legs. She couldn't pinpoint why she was attracted. Maybe it was his calm yet articulate voice. His eyes seemed to read her deepest thoughts. Whatever the cause, the effect had her wrestling with sparks of passion that consumed her previous apprehension.

At least for tonight, she would not think about how each zero in the Utopia 40 prize was like carrying everyone else's lost dream.

She drank more wine and became less concerned about her dress being too short. At length, she could barely hang on to the thought of Utopia. Peter led her to a narrow dark hallway.

"What's on your mind," he asked with a rich voice devoid of emotion.

"I am feeling woozy, yet filled with ..."

"What?"

"Passion. I need to be careful of the devil on the prowl," she mumbled incoherently.

When she nearly fainted, he lifted her with ease. She burrowed her faced against his neck; up close his fair complexion was a contrast to her tanned skin.

"You are perfection—beautiful and broken," he whispered. His eyes were like dark tunnels to an unknown universe, a journey worth taking.

The memory of Utopia 40 floated away as Peter proceeded to plow his fangs into her neck. Her vision faded and reemerged into a kaleidoscope of images. She lost track of time and space; one moment they were standing together on the cliff of the Marin Headlands, and the next she was lying on the grand piano while he played, the vibrations of the keys rippled throughout her body.

The following morning, the sunlight woke Leslie and she found herself lying partially nude on her sofa. Peter was gone. She felt defiled, but the passion continued to pulse in her blood. She ran to retrieve the Bible from the dark corner of the closet. An electrical shock stunned her body and knocked the wind out of her. After a few minutes of recovery, she tried her other hand and an excruciating burning sensation made it smoke.

And then it hit her, the one impossible reason why she couldn't retrieve the winning ticket. The Bible was untouchable because she had become a vampire.

$$\star\star\star$$

A year later, Emma appeared at The Sisters of Adoration church requesting Sister Anne. She found the nun's information in the inner cover of the Bible and felt compelled to return the book after a new neighbor discovered it in Leslie's former apartment. Sister Anne asked if Emma would like to keep it, but she politely declined.

After she departed, Sister Anne intuitively flipped through the Bible and found a palm leaf cross burned at the edges as well as a singed ticket. She could barely make out the numbers or signature, as the ticket was smeared in soot. The Bible's pages remained pristine, so she placed the cross back in its spot. She held the ticket above the lit candles and let it catch fire and burn. The smoke rose and intermingled with the perpetual prayers.

Marin

I WISHED I HADN'T COME, but the mixed scent of apple cinnamon lured me into staying. A line of strangers sat at a long table in a roped off area of a Sacramento restaurant. Sun streamed through a side window. I squeezed between two people fidgeting near the end of the table until a man in a blue suit stood up.

"Welcome," he said. "I'm Blaine and we're here to celebrate Aunt Marge."

Aunt Marge, I groaned to myself, wishing I could exit. Was this the cranky Marge I'd known?

"I'm her nephew," said Blaine, sweeping his gaze over the people gathered, "Judging by all of you, Aunt Marge had many friends."

Around the table, postures changed, chairs squeaked, and throats cleared, suggesting that others remembered Marge as I did.

WHERE'S GEORGE?
Kimberly A. Edwards

"We flew in from Florida to handle her affairs," said Blaine. A grey-haired woman in a sequined sweater joined him. "My wife Helen," he said. She nodded, we nodded. "Nice of you all to come," he said. "We'd like to hear from you; how you knew Marge."

I groused at myself for getting trapped; what could I possibly offer? I'd seen Marge only once in the last thirty years and I wasn't good at masking the truth.

Blaine picked up a glass of water. As he pressed his lips to the rim, accolades from the guests began down the table: "She came to our crochet club every week," "She was so tiny," "No one could bowl like her," were among the testimonials.

By the time my turn came, I knew that I had known Marge the longest. "I met her as a child," I said, aware of 30 sets of eyes on me. "She was my parents' friend."

In fact, in the early 1950s, my parents belonged to a church where they met a childless couple. Marge was the wife. The husband, George. Every Tuesday night the four of them went out to dinner. When my mother entered a long period of illness, the couple continued to visit our home.

With cinnamon scent stirring compassion, I grasped every platitude I could muster, flinging them out to the group: Marge's hair was always tidy, she loved dogs, she spoke in a soft tone. I wasn't about to tell them about her husband's last plane ride with my dad.

"Nice," said Blaine.

"Ooh," said guests around the table.

"Hmmm," said Blaine's wife Helen, pulling her sweater together as it caught the light.

What I didn't say was that Marge was a chronic complainer. Her eyebrows arched in review of life. She sent her food back in every restaurant. The liver and onions were cold, cabbage overdone, coffee cup dirty. She hounded waitress and manager alike. Thankfully, Marge was always polite to me. After my mother died, she would say, "Your mother was the most beautiful person. I loved your mother." There were no sweeter words to me, and for this reason, I begrudgingly accepted Marge.

Meanwhile, Marge's husband George was a mild-mannered man, as was necessary to tolerate a difficult spouse. He was easily given to smiles and a nervous laugh, especially between cigarettes. George was the friend my dad could rely on to join him in any activity. They shared airplane shows, car exhibits, motorcycle rides, and golf games. They watched over each other like brothers.

Blaine took another sip of water. "We've been going through Aunt Marge's house, learning much about her." He exchanged glances with wife Helen, a faint chuckle escaping her lip. "But enough of that. Would everyone please sign the memory book at the back of the room?" He motioned to a corner display. "And please enjoy our photos of Marge and her life."

Based on the squirming bodies around me, I sensed that more was known than was being voiced around the table. No face gave a hint, yet repositioning elbows told the story of tales we were not telling. I picked up my purse, intending to leave after signing the book. There was no more I could do for Marge, wherever she was.

Upon penning my name in the book, I glanced at the photos: Marge as a girl with dogs, in hat and gloves, and with George. The minute I saw him, the George of my childhood reeled before me: saying hello, tipping his golf hat, waving as he took off with Dad for another adventure. I lingered in these thoughts, as if contemplation could bring those days back. Where had the years gone?

"So, you knew Marge from a long time ago," said Blaine. He'd followed me over to the table, sensing that I carried some history, the kind we know but don't always share.

"I didn't know her well," I said, feeling his stare combing my face. "But she was always nice." I omitted the fact that she wasn't particularly nice to most people.

Crow's feet lined Blaine's eyes, red at the edges. "She hung onto everything," he said, signaling to his wife.

"A hoarder," said Helen, who closed in. "A hoarder who shared nothing."

"We've been going through all her junk," said Blaine, lowering his voice. "Cards, letters, newspaper clippings dated back in the 1950s."

Helen rolled her eyes. "She was so secretive. We never knew a thing about her husband George," she whispered.

"My dad's best friend," I proffered. No harm in passing along facts, since Marge had no children. I was beginning to feel sucked in, as if relating the past was my duty.

Blaine raised his brow. "Uncle George? We've been looking all over for him after finding a Neptune Society receipt on Marge's dining room table."

"There in her piles," said Helen. "He's got to be there. We know she didn't just get rid of him."

"He could be under any stack," said Blaine."

"So much to look through," sighed Helen. She put her hand to her temple.

As I saw the drain on Helen, my memory flashed to my dad. Years earlier, he told me that George was diagnosed with lung cancer. When George could no longer play golf, Dad took him up in his plane. Wearing their golf hats, they rose into the blue sky. They flew over grey and brown farmhouses, orchards and vineyards, slopes leading to the ocean, where redwoods stood up to gales blowing in from the Pacific.

"Beautiful," said Blaine, upon hearing this account.

I picked around in my head for more recollections. One by one they loosened. When George died, Marge approached Dad with a request. Would he spread George's ashes off the coast? What would Dad not do for his friend of many years! He jumped into the task, securing the required permit. Then he practiced how he would pack George's ashes into a 30-inch cardboard poster tube, protracted from the plane window. At just the right moment, he would release the ashes.

As these memories arose, I held them, stroked them, felt around for more. On the anticipated day, Dad and another friend, both in golf caps, boarded Dad's Cessna with the tube of ashes. As the plane climbed, the view opened to fields, orchards, and slopes rolling west. The fog that sometimes blurred the landscape had thinned to reveal the contours of all that was real and true.

As the plane approached the coast, precipitation began to collect along the rim of the windshield. Dad signaled the friend to unlatch the window. The friend poked the tube into the atmosphere. Ashes wiggled out in a perfect steady flow. That is, until the battering wind bent the tube.

"Hey!" shouted the friend over the trill of the propeller. "Something's wrong. Ashes stuck in the tube."

"Then we'll have to blast George out," hollered Dad.

Applying his foot to the pedals and hands to controls, Dad took command of maneuvers, pulling and pushing in collusion with nose, wings, and tail. As the plane climbed, dipped, and banked, the drill influenced the airflow at just the right angle. With the tube taking a beating, it straightened, releasing George's remains. But the fragments, instead of drifting off, flew back into the cockpit, powdering Dad.

Dad recounted this scene to me that night, describing what he called "our efforts to liberate" George. "He just didn't want to leave us pals," said Dad, half-laughing half-cheering. "We tried our hardest, but he came whooshing back in."

"Do you think I should tell Marge what happened?" asked Dad.

"Absolutely not," I said, as only a daughter can.

Now in the Sacramento restaurant facing Blaine's and Helen's despair, their pleas pressed into me. "If you know what she did with George," said Blaine, "please tell us."

What could I say? I was proud of Dad's efforts. I was also proud of George. In my head, the two buddies were together again. Yet as the sole survivor of this story, I felt the weight of a curious burden: telling the relatives where George was—

or wasn't. I drew my arms around him in my mind and for a moment, I felt like his daughter, too.

"He's in the perfect place," I said. "My dad took him up to spread his ashes."

"What!" said Blaine.

My brain whizzed through ways to soften the truth. "He took him to the coast in his plane," I said. I couldn't bring myself to spoil the message by disclosing the botched delivery.

"Thank God!" said Blaine, sinking his head into his hands. "She could have stuck him anywhere, and she put him in the Pacific Ocean."

"At rest on the waves," said Helen. She brought her palms together. Her cheeks relaxed, as did Blaine's.

Truly," I said, wondering if this were the right word. Is skipping particulars still telling the truth? Are right and truth the same? Is truth, like friendship, fathers, and memorial services, never perfectly replicated?

In that moment I knew that truth and right were not the same, but close enough. Seeing the relief on Blaine and Helen's faces, I knew that I had taken George from memory and placed him where he belonged.

Sacramento

Cemetary photo by Jill Hedgecock

FIVE-YEAR-OLD **RILEY O'ROARKE SNUGGLED** with her favorite toy, a stuffed dragon. She burrowed in, pretending the bitter odor permeating the hospital room was her dragon flaming the bad blood from her body. Six months ago, on her first hospital stay, Da had presented Riley with the velvety blue dragon with silver wings. And Riley fell in love.

"What's her name?" Riley's soft voice had asked.

"Dochas. It means hope in Irish Gaelic," Da said.

Riley rolled the unfamiliar word around her tongue — Doe-haas.

"She's to bring ye strength and hope for yer swift recovery." Da ruffled Riley's hair before he bent down and kissed the top of her head. She used to have dark brown curls like Da. That was before her hair had grown brittle and covered her pillow every morning until there was none left.

DO DRAGONS GO TO HEAVEN?
Jordan Bernal

A soft rustle in the dim, private room drew Riley's attention. Mum mumbled in her sleep as she shifted in the lounge chair. The only light came from the reds, yellows, and greens of the monitors.

Riley's thoughts turned to the day before. She hadn't felt well at breakfast but didn't say anything that might spoil the day. The picnic her parents planned was to be the first family outing since her diagnosis. A time to have fun again. To forget the sadness that crept into Da's eyes all too often.

The sun had warmed her, pushing back the cold that never seemed to go away. During a short hike, Da had pointed out all sorts of gross bugs—but that was before. Before she grew tired and shaky. Before her arms and legs ached. Before she crumbled to the forest floor.

Once at the hospital, Riley had been taken for endless tests and poked with needles. Afterward, the grim-faced emergency room doctor told Riley's parents she had developed a serious infection. She needed to be admitted and given a strong dose of antibiotics.

"I don't want ants, bats, and ticks inside me," Riley told the doctor. She grabbed Da's hand and pleaded. "You said ticks were nasty buggers when they burrowed into Buddy's fur last year. We took him to the doggie doctor. Do you remember? Don't let them put bugs in me."

"No, my precious. Not ants, bats, and ticks. Antibiotics." Da reassured her.

"It's medicine to get the infection—the germs—out of yer body."

As soon as she was settled in the pediatric wing, the doctors huddled with Mum and Da in the corner. They must have thought Riley couldn't hear their whispers, but even though she was very sick, her ears still worked fine.

"After the antibiotic treatment, we'll start another round of chemotherapy," the doctor said as she scanned Riley's chart. "Her leukemia's back, more aggressive than before. Let's hope a bone marrow donor is found, and soon. Has your entire family been tested?"

"Your brother?" Mum whispered to Da. "He's all that's left."

Da's normally ruddy face paled. "I can't . . . we haven't spoken since . . .." He squeezed his eyes closed. "I didn't even go back home when our parents died. Why would he help us?"

"That doesn't matter now," Mum interrupted. "Please," she pleaded.

Da shoved a shaky hand through his hair. "He won't forgive me for leaving the family farm and stealing ye away from him."

"You didn't." Mum placed her hand gently on Da's forearm. "The only thing you stole was my heart. We fell in love. Your brother will understand. You need to try. For our daughter's sake."

"Where's this brother?" The doctor raised her voice. When Da didn't respond, the doctor crossed her arms and scowled. "You need to reconcile with him. Quickly. Especially as he might be Riley's best hope."

Da stared at the floor, his shoulders hunched. Finally, he nodded. He grabbed his coat and rushed from the room without saying a word to Riley. Everything seemed urgent now that she had returned to the hospital.

After Da left, Riley asked, "Will I go to heaven and meet God when I die?"

Mum held her cross necklace near her bare lips, mumbled a prayer, and kissed the gold symbol of faith before she took a deep breath and schooled her features. "Of course, but that's a long way off, so don't worry about that now. You need to rest and build up your strength."

Riley closed her eyes and drifted into a light sleep.

The faint beep-beep-beep kept pace with Riley's shallow breaths and woke her.

"Mommy," Riley whispered into the slowly brightening room. She hugged Dochas closer, and a coughing fit wracked Riley's body.

"Yes, my love. Are you thirsty?" The sound of Mum's heels clicking on the linoleum reverberated against the quiet.

Mum raised the head of the bed and held the plastic cup with the bendy straw to Riley's lips.

Riley wasn't thirsty but took a sip anyway.

"Mommy, where do dragons go to die? Do dragons go to heaven? I want

Dochas to be with me always."

Mum sighed and set the cup aside. She sat on the edge of the bed and took Riley's hand. "Let me tell you a story my grandfather told me when I was a wee girl not much older than you are now."

Riley settled Dochas across her chest, the stuffed dragon's triangular head resting over Riley's heart, as if protecting her.

"There's a magical place called Ireland that's full of wonders and special creatures. Faeries, leprechauns, and dragons."

"Isn't Ireland where Da was born?"

"Yes, and my parents as well. I met your da there, and we fell in love, but that's a story for another day."

"Promise?"

Mum nodded, then continued in her best story voice. "Grandfather told me the tale of an old dragon—Quinn was his name—who had roamed the world for centuries. Quinn loved to fly and visit wondrous places—like the Great Wall of China, erupting volcanoes in Hawaii, and the Great Barrier Reef in Australia. But his favorite place was the rolling green hills and sheer cliffs of his magical homeland—Ireland."

"Will I get to see the magic of Ireland someday?"

"Oh, honey. I sure hope so." Mum fought back tears. "Anyway, one day Quinn was soaring on the warm air currents over the pyramids of Giza when suddenly he faltered. He should have fallen amidst the massive stone structures far below, but he called on his magical powers and righted himself just in the nick of time."

"Did he fall because he was weak like me?"

"Sort of." Mum caressed Riley's cheek, then continued the story. "Quinn realized his magic was failing. His old wings were ragged and torn, and his once diamond-bright scales were dull and cracked. So he made his way over land and water toward home. Though the journey was slow, his indomitable spirit kept him flying ever onward."

"What's in . . . inbomable?"

"Indomitable. It means invincible, impossible to defeat. You see, Quinn had an important mission. It was vital that he return to his magical land to pass on his indomitable spirit to a sick lass that needed special magic to cure her. Once Quinn willingly gave his spirit away to the young girl, he chose his favorite location in the heart of Ireland and his body transformed into a grassy hillock."

The story made Riley sad and yet pleased at the same time. She swiped at a lone tear that rolled down her cheek. "Does that mean Quinn wasn't allowed in heaven?"

"Oh, no. By giving away his spirit, Quinn showed the full expanse of his love, and God welcomed Quinn with open arms."

"But . . . wasn't his body still in Ireland? How did he get to heaven?"

Mum clasped a hand to her heart. "Our bodies don't go to heaven. Our soul—our spirit and heart do."

Riley was still confused. "But didn't he give his inbomable spirit to the sick girl?"

"Yes, and because of Quinn's unselfishness, God allowed Quinn's spirit to be in two places at once. In the sick lass and in heaven."

"What happened to the girl?" Riley yawned, weary to the bone.

"She grew to be a fine young woman. She devoted her life to caring for other sick children. And so, Quinn's spirit lived on." Mum leaned over and kissed Riley's forehead. "Rest now, my love. You need to save your strength."

Though her eyes burned and felt scratchy, Riley closed them. The beep-beep-beep of the monitors lulled her to sleep. And Riley dreamed. She dreamed of flying on the back of Dochas across America and over the vast, blue ocean. They landed in a checkerboard-patterned green field with stacked-stone walls surrounding an enormous grass-covered hillock. Tangy smoke from a nearby farmhouse scented the air.

Riley climbed over the wall as the cool, spring wind spoke to her. "Ye must believe in the magic for it to come to ye."

"I do believe … with all my heart," Riley replied. "But even if I don't get well, please make sure my dragon goes to heaven. She's my best friend."

Lighthearted and full of energy, Riley skipped along the hillock, picked wildflowers, and raised her face to the warmth of the sun. All too soon Dochas beckoned. Riley climbed onto her dragon's back, and together they soared above Ireland. Riley gazed upon the rolling green hills and craggy cliffs, the colorful buildings that dotted the quays of the fishing villages, and the busy roadways intersecting the cities.

Riley woke later that night to the continuous drone of the hospital.

"Mommy, where did Da go?"

"He went to find your own magical dragon that will help you fight this terrible disease. A dragon to give you his indomitable spirit and good bone marrow."

Riley smiled and hugged Dochas tight. "I have my dragon. And I believe." Her voice faded as she drifted back to sleep.

✭✭✭

The next time Riley opened her eyes, sunlight streamed through the window. She squinted and spotted Da with another man standing next to her bed. The man looked a lot like Da, but without the sad eyes and constant frown. And he held Dochas.

"My treasure." Da kissed her forehead. "This is my brother, yer Uncle Quinn. He'll be giving ye some of his bone marrow. And ye'll be better."

"Will he go to heaven like Quinn the Dragon in Mommy's story?"

Da glanced at Mum and smiled. "Ah, she told ye that tale, did she? It's one of my favorites."

Riley nodded.

"Well, Uncle Quinn will undoubtedly go to heaven someday, but not for a long time yet—I hope." Da draped his arm over his brother's shoulder, and the sadness that had been in Da's eyes for months disappeared.

"I'm glad yer da came to find me. Because me and this special dragon here are gonna make ye well." Quinn tucked Dochas against Riley's side. "Do ye think we might be friends?"

"Are you and Da friends again?" At Quinn's nod, Riley reached for his hand. "Then yes, we can. 'Cause, he didn't mean to steal Mommy from you."

At Mum's gasp, Uncle Quinn brushed the back of his fingers over Riley's cheek. "I know, my sweeting. It was a misunderstanding is all. The important thing is we're all together again. A family. And family is magical."

Riley snuggled with Dochas as her family gathered around. "Good. And I'll get well because … I believe and I have my special hope."

Tri-Valley

JAMES VEECH

Almaz Ayana,
in the Style of Billy Collins
[Almaz set a 10,000m women's world record in the 2016 Olympic Games]

The small Ethiopian would win,
I knew it the minute I saw her head-erect posture
and graceful stride that even gazelles would envy.

If the crowd were to hush, if the stadium went still
if all the other runners were to stop dead
to admire the short piston stroke of her arms,

her quiet upper body, the fine-tuned legs,
you would hear no sound at all
because her small feet brushed the track like a quiet caress.

Did she arise on race day with thoughts of laurel garlands?
Or was the force of her running the ancient instinct horses have
to catch and pass the one ahead?

Perhaps her mind was in Addis Ababa,
wondering about her child,
and her body was running by itself without thought
as long as she felt the familiar lightness of her effort.
No one was her equal on the track that day.

The pace of the pack slowed her at first
but stride by stride she strained against the invisible bond
     holding her back
until it broke and she ran alone,
like the days of her childhood on red African clay.

The moment she broke free
so my spirit did too. It lifted to the track.
and ran next to her stride for stride,

reminding me of days at the beach
when I used to run
where the waves had wet the sand,

and there I was, a running machine,
determined to be the first to cross
the imaginary finish line.

SF/Peninsula

BEFORE

I remember my niece Catie, before Batten disease took her. I remember her in snapshots.

Thanksgiving Day at my brother Joe's house. A scarecrow rested on a bale of hay on the front porch, one half of his overalls unbuttoned and drooping over his yellow-and-blue-checked flannel shirt. Garlands of autumn leaves adorned the mantle and stair railings. Joe's wife, Korky, was craftsy. As a stay-at-home mom with four kids ("and hopefully more to come, it's in God's hands," she'd say), she was the first to admit that she and my brother tried to live a 1950s life in the 1990s.

IN THE GRIP
Marianne Lonsdale

Catie played tag with my husband, her Uncle Michael. He was extra special to her because they shared the same birthday. Michael wore a small diamond stud in one ear. She teased him about nine times that day that men do not wear earrings.

Catie darted around parked cars in the cul de sac. Her head turned back every few seconds to check how close Michael was to catching her. Her features weren't beautiful, but they captivated. The energy, the life in that little heart-shaped face, the excitement. Catie was up for anything.

I didn't see anything lurking but Korky did. When she could keep the heebie-jeebies at bay, when she didn't go to that dark worry place that mothers sometimes can't avoid, she thought her third child might have some learning disabilities. But sometimes Korky feared something worse.

INTO THE DARK

Catie started losing her vision at age nine and was blind by eleven. The doctors blamed some eye disease whose name I no longer remember. Dealing just with blindness seems simple now.

A teacher came to their home twice a week to teach her Braille and living skills like how to navigate with a white cane. Blindness was horrible but manageable.

The summer Catie was eleven, our families rented a cabin in the Sierras. Joe and Korky had six children now, and Michael and I had a son, Nick, four years old. Catie quickly figured out the layout of the cabin, and was able, without help, to go upstairs to her bedroom and downstairs to the family room with the ping-pong table.

But she often lashed out in anger because she couldn't play like her sisters could. Ping-pong balls bounced past her or off her. She couldn't run around outdoors. Uneven ground, boulders, and trees blocked her way. The same natural obstacles that made running around fun for her sisters and Nick were dangerous for Catie. Her frustration spilled into tears and tantrums.

Korky and I went into town one bright hot day for shopping and lunch, ready for a few hours without kids or husbands. Catie was upset. We wouldn't take her with us, and she couldn't ride bikes and scooters with Nick and her sisters. Nothing worked for her.

Uncle Michael came to the rescue. He drove Catie and the other kids to the Stanislaus River. Michael led Catie along a flat wide trail, Catie scanning the ground with her cane for rocks and uneven patches. And then they fished. A red-letter day for Catie. That she caught nothing was of no importance.

Little Annie, the baby of Joe and Korky's family, was two and a half that summer. In my snapshot of Annie that week, she is on her belly on a skateboard, zooming across the wood deck with the same impish look that used to be on Catie's face.

THE DIAGNOSIS

Catie started having frequent seizures. Some so slight they could only be seen on brain scans, while others caused violent convulsions. Her cognitive and physical abilities were below average.

A degenerative disease seemed to be progressing. A team of doctors, puzzled by her array of symptoms, worked to diagnose her condition. Catie was thirteen before she was diagnosed with Batten disease.

> "Over time, affected children suffer mental impairment, worsening seizures, and progressive loss of sight and motor skills. Eventually, children with Batten disease become blind, bedridden, and unable to communicate and presently is always fatal. Batten disease is not contagious or, at this time, preventable."
> *From the website of the Batten disease & Research Association (BDSRA)*

This was unreal. This monster disease found life when both parents carried a rare defective gene. The odds of two people with this gene coming together were low.

> "Batten disease is relatively rare, occurring in an estimated 2 to 4 of every 100,000 births in the United States. Although classified as a rare disease, it often strikes more than one person in families that carry the defective gene."

More than one person? Oh my god, who else?

> "The disease begins between ages 2 and 8. Typical early signs are loss of muscle coordination and seizures along with progressive mental deterioration."

Joe and Korky's other kids were over eight and no signs. Except Annie, impish Annie, four years old. Nick was six, but I didn't believe for a second that he had Batten. Nick was near perfect. And the odds were on my side—fat chance that I was a carrier and had also married one. I felt guilty for my relief.

The doctors drew blood samples from Annie. The lab back east, across the country, the only lab that tested for Batten, lost her samples and the process began again. Annie's diagnosis took a year. By the time Batten was confirmed, the original neurologist had left and the new one wanted to start from scratch. He doubted the Batten diagnosis, wanted to resample, retest, do it all over. Joe and Korky refused. By then they were Batten experts, attending conferences, joining on-line support groups. My brother and his wife knew more about the disease than this doctor. More tests would not force the monster to leave their home.

TELLING NICK

I was driving with Nick to Target when he asked about his cousin Catie. Nick adored his cousins. They were the closest he was going to get to having siblings.

"What's going to happen to Catie when she grows up?" Nick piped up from the back, still too small to sit in the front seat. At eight, he was just about big enough to stop using a booster seat.

I'd been wrestling with when to tell him more about Catie.

"Will she get a job?" Nick asked. "Or will someone still have to take care of her?"

"Her mom and dad will always take care of her," I said. My first instinct was to assure him that everything would be all right.

But it wouldn't be all right ever again. How honest should I be? Nick had seen Batten destroying Catie—blinding her, shutting down her brain, turning her muscles to mush. But he didn't know that children with the disease don't survive their teens.

"Honey, kids with Batten don't live long lives. They don't usually make it past their teenage years."

A guttural wail poured from him, a sound unlike any I'd ever heard from my boy. He sobbed, his whole body rocking forward and back. I pulled over, climbed into the back seat and pulled Nick to me. He calmed a bit. He slid his hand up my sleeve and rubbed my arm. Leaned his head on my shoulder.

"What's happening with Catie is one of the worst things you'll ever have to deal with." I winced, wondering if I should have just thrown the information at him like that. "Honey, I am so sorry."

Nick said no more about Catie until a week later, when I was reading to him at bedtime. His hand closed the book I held. His blue-grey eyes were moist.

"I keep thinking about Catie. At school, at baseball practice, all the time."

"I think about her a lot too," I said.

Nick nodded, his mouth trembling. His hand tugged at the elastic waist of his blue flannel pj pants, patterned with bouncing soccer balls.

"You can talk to me or Daddy about Catie anytime."

His teary eyes closed. Oh god, I missed Catie already, and I ached for Nick, who was going to lose his cousin and attend her funeral, this year or the next.

SPAGHETTI DINNER

My family filled four long folding tables in the gym of Saint Veronica's. My six brothers, my sister, our spouses and children, my mother and father. Catie was strapped into her wheelchair, her head drooping forward, at the top of our row of tables, in the place of honor. Joe sat to her left.

Servers brought steaming bowls of spaghetti, two for each table, one with red sauce and one with pesto. Plates of garlic bread, loaded with butter and paprika, were already on the table, along with antipasto platters of celery, carrots, and olives. Two cousins had organized a dinner as a fundraiser for Batten disease research. The dinner was sold out. And the people kept coming.

Joe was like the Godfather, with men lined up to see him. The story of his girls had struck deep. All these men that I remembered as boys kept streaming in. Men who loved my easygoing brother, who had played baseball with him, had gone to high school with him. They lined up in front of Joe, each spending a few minutes saying how sorry they were. Doing that manly teasing thing. Lots of conversations started with "remember that time…"

I couldn't take it. I wanted to cry and I wanted to scream. My son and his young cousins were restless. I took the kids outside to the schoolyard to run off some energy.

The dinner raised $11,000. What could I do? Near strangers were throwing dinners while I allowed the shock of the disease to paralyze me. I wasn't doing enough.

Korky spoke to the group. She used to be terrified of public speaking but now held audiences rapt. She explained the disease and talked about living with children with Batten. She finished by talking about her other children.

"I've spoken a lot about my daughters Catie and Annie. I need to also talk about my other children—Tony, Kelly, Kerri, and Amy. These four are my heroes. These four children are in the trenches every day, taking care of their sisters, giving a life of service to the cause. I need to thank these heroes."

Korky is my hero.

HOLY WATER

My parents became convinced that the answer was Lourdes, the grotto in France where some people believe the Virgin Mary appeared to a young girl, Bernadette, in 1858. The holy site where miracle cures occur.

Not just anyone gets dipped in the waters. Candidates must apply to the Catholic Church, be selected, and then pray like crazy that once they get there the waters work. My parents begged my brother and his wife to apply.

Joe and Korky debated whether to complete the paperwork. They were not Catholics. They were Christians, members of a small independent church. I thought the powers of Lourdes were a fantasy. I'd loved the story of Bernadette and the Virgin apparitions when I was a young girl. But if I were Joe and Korky, I'd probably fly to Lourdes in a nanosecond. I'd try every cockamamie cure I could find.

Korky became intrigued with the idea of traveling to Lourdes on a pilgrimage, a journey of devotion to Jesus. Even if they went and the girls were not cured, the pilgrimage might be worthwhile. But how to explain to their four healthy kids that they couldn't afford to take them to Europe?

Joe and Korky decided to apply. They filled out forms in triplicate, obtained doctor statements, and included pictures.

Months passed. Planning even though they were trying not to plan. Hoping for a cure, couldn't help hoping. The answer finally arrived. So many more people were applying than Lourdes could handle that the Church was now limiting acceptances to Catholics.

VISITS

Kerri and Amy, two of Catie's younger sisters, bounced into our house. They were fifteen and twelve now, and Nick was ten. He ran down the stairs, waving to them to follow, showing where he'd already set up sleeping bags in our family room.

Nick ran back upstairs to his bedroom and grabbed a plastic container stuffed with money.

"I saved this for Batten disease research," he told the girls as he leapt back down the stairs, covering two at a time. "$58.50." For months my son had saved half his allowance as well as money he'd earned pet sitting for neighbors.

Kerri, who went from child to teen to mother hen in a flash, took the container and set it on top of her suitcase. The three cousins hugged. Amy wiped away a tear.

"Do you want to ride bikes?" Amy asked. The moment had passed. My nieces could block the Batten monster from taking over my house.

Kerri and Amy are such terrific girls. With so much to bear. They love Catie and Annie, but they get frustrated and angry about the attention demanded by the care of their disabled sisters. And then they cry with guilt over their anger. At our house, they can just hang, just chill for a few days.

MOTHER'S DAY

Caitlin Rose died in 2012 on Mother's Day. She took her last breath in her mother's arms. She was twenty-two, an elder of the Batten community. Nick, then a gangly fifteen-year-old, hung out with Catie that weekend. On the day Catie died, Nick said good-bye, kissed her and rubbed her shoulders. As always, she smiled.

TODAY

Annie is twenty-one. She sleeps away most of her days. She wears diapers. She sometimes walks but is mostly in her wheelchair. She is spoon-fed on good days. A tube put in her stomach last summer keeps her fed and medicated on bad days. She is in her waning stages. Sometimes when Annie is alert, she sits in a big easy chair in the living room or strapped into her wheelchair. When she's alert, she is joyful. It's hard to explain but she smiles and laughs, and I feel joy from her.

AFTER

There will be no after Batten. Even when Annie is gone, the disease will remain with us. We grieve continuously. I detach for hours, for days at a time. Then it will hit me. I'll be walking down the street and my gut will clench, and the tears will rise hot through my cheeks and flood my face. I never feel like I'm doing enough for Joe and Korky's family.

Yes, we have a stronger sense of how important every day is. A stronger sense that today is all we have. But that gift is just not worth it. I'd give up pretty much anything to go back to life before Batten. Before the loss of innocence. Before our children found out monsters are real. Before we were in the grip.

Mt. Diablo

ON A BALMY AFTERNOON IN THE SPRING of

1907, Hawaii's local legend, George Freeth, was "discovered" by the famous author, Jack London. Hawaii was the first stop on London's sailing journey that would take him to exotic locations throughout the South Seas. In a story London wrote several years later, entitled "Surfing: A Royal Sport, from the Cruise of the Snark," he described sitting on Waikiki Beach watching surfers riding on the waves. That was the first time he saw the amazing George Freeth, calling him a "brown-skinned Greek god." He wrote that the young man stood erect on his surfboard, "...flying through the air, flying forward, flying fast as the surge on which he stands. He is Mercury...His heels are winged and in them is the swiftness of the sea."

Needless to say, Jack London was thoroughly impressed with the young Hawaiian athlete. Determined to learn to ride on surfboard himself, London spent two days attempting to learn the sport on his own. And he failed. Now famous all over the world, London wasn't accustomed to being unsuccessful at things he wanted to do. Surfing, like most other sports, requires a great deal of practice, and from his writings, we know the author-turned-adventurer wasn't happy with his lack of progress. When London's friend and fellow writer, Alexander Hume Ford, offered to give him lessons, he gladly accepted. The next day, Ford and the surfer that London had admired so greatly, George Freeth, agreed to show London the proper technique of surf-riding. London describes their efforts to teach him to ride the "big waves." After tumbling from his board, fighting his way up through countless feet of water and white froth, he "finally tackled surf-riding."

✯✯✯

Centuries ago, the sport of surfing was born upon Hawaii's turquoise breakers. Once a pastime enjoyed by Hawaiian royalty, it was nearly snuffed out by puritanical New England missionaries who arrived in the Islands in the early 1800s. Over the ensuing decades, the well-meaning missionaries did their best to obliterate the Hawaiian culture. When it came to surfboard riding, they considered it a frivolous waste of time, and the scanty "bathing suits" indecent. Ironically, by the end of the 19th century many grandsons of the very missionaries who had tried to ban the sport were among the Islands' best surfers. They rode the breakers at the ever-popular Waikiki Beach, shoulder to shoulder with the Hawaiian boys whose ancestors had created the leisure activity.

The true revival of surfboard riding began in Hawaii around 1900 when

GEORGE FREETH:
FATHER OF CALIFORNIA SURFING
Colleen Fliedner

Waves on Woodland Beach, photo by Suzy Orpin, Mt. Diablo

Freeth created a thinner, lighter version of the traditional sixteen-foot-long Hawaiian "*olo olo*." Though the new boards resembled a coffin lid, they were shorter and allowed the rider to cut across a wave's curl at an angle, rather than simply riding it into shore on the wash.

Born on the Island of Oahu in 1883, George Freeth was the grandson of Hawaii's Minister of Foreign Affairs, British born William Green, and Hawaiian Elizabeth "Lepeka" Kahalaunani. Growing up near Waikiki Beach, Freeth spent much of his childhood in the water. By the time he was in his late teens, Freeth is said to have "ruled the waves." The handsome young athlete was also famous throughout the Islands as a champion water-polo player, diver, and swimmer.

In 1911, Freeth headed for Southern California to surf. With his good looks and muscular body, he was a real crowd pleaser. Girls swooned and young men wanted to be like him. It didn't take long for business tycoon and real estate developer, Henry E. Huntington, to hear about the amazing young man from Hawaii who "walked on water." Huntington hired Freeth to perform his surf riding feats in Redondo Beach—not the least of which was riding a wave while standing on his head. Huntington owned about 90% of the property in the beach town and believed that the surfer could attract potential land buyers to the area by offering these intriguing exhibitions twice daily.

Not only was "the Hawaiian Wonder" a hit when it came to drawing people to Mr. Huntington's fledging seaside community, boys from around the southland flocked to Freeth to learn how to surf. He was happy to mentor these boys, though he foolishly did it free of charge. Money troubles would, in fact, plague George Freeth the rest of his life. And yet, he willingly shared his skills with the boys and even a few girls who idolized him.

Meanwhile, Abbott Kinney, who developed Venice Beach, took Huntington's cue and hired George to draw potential buyers to his own beachfront. Although performing his "surfing act" at both beaches required him to continually make the twelve-mile trip between Redondo and Venice, the Hawaiian needed the money to make ends meet. When he wasn't surfing, Freeth was a lifeguard, and a swimming and diving instructor at various plunges (huge public swimming pools that were popular in that era). Ever the showman, he loved to demonstrate his skills on the diving board. His fancy flips and double twists became legendary.

Freeth's greatest achievement was his innovative approach to lifeguarding. Shortly after arriving in California, he took up the cause that was nearest and dearest to his heart: revamping the entire system of water rescues. Not only did he revolutionize the lifeguards' techniques, he personally saved hundreds of lives. Believe it or not, Freeth's concept of swimming to bathers in distress was a new one. Lifeguards, then called "lifesavers," consisted of volunteers who launched a small rescue boat into the waves and rowed to assist a drowning swimmer. By the time they reached the victim, it was usually too late. Freeth felt there should be a trained, paid work force to "guard" the beaches, especially during the crowded summer months. Instead of wasting precious time to round up volunteers and launch a boat, he believed that professional lifeguards should simply dive into the surf and swim to the victim in order to accomplish a faster rescue. The boat could be used for back-up purposes. Another innovation was the "torpedo buoy," which would assist lifeguards and victims alike. Working with a friend, he developed a torpedo-shaped, floating pod—the prototype for lifesaving equipment that is still used by lifeguards today.

Within five months of his arrival in California, he was appointed as the "captain" of the newly formed "Venice Lifesaving Crew," the first professionally trained lifeguards in history. Not only did he instruct the men in the method of "rescue swimming," Freeth taught them to utilize the strength of the rip currents to reach a swimmer in distress more quickly. Up to that point, rescue personnel, like the volunteer lifesavers on the East Coast, believed that rip currents dragged a swimmer under (hence, the term "undertow"). Freeth knew this wasn't true. He showed his pupils how to work with—instead of against—the deadly current; and to use its natural force to guide them back to shore. Now a standard practice, countless thousands of lives have been saved through the years by employing Freeth's techniques.

In December of 1908, a winter storm suddenly moved into Santa Monica Bay, catching several Japanese fishing boats off guard. The small boats floundered near the breakwater, finally capsizing. When word of the accident reached Freeth, he dashed down to the Venice Pier. While dozens of men stood by helplessly watching the drama unfold, Freeth braved the churning waves and gale force winds and dove into the frigid water. One by one, he single-handedly rescued the fishermen. He had already saved seven men when the team he had trained in life-saving techniques saved the other three. Word about the life and death event spread rapid-fire throughout Venice, and thousands gathered to see George Freeth's miraculous rescues. Newspapers grabbed the story, bringing Freeth and his lifeguards into the national spotlight. As a result of his heroism, George Freeth was awarded the Congressional Gold Medal of Honor, the highest honor a civilian can receive from the U. S. government. When he was given this award in 1910, he was only the fifth person to have received it since George Washington was so honored in 1776.

In 1913, Freeth was hired to work at the prestigious Los Angeles Athletic Club, where he coached numerous swimmers and divers who would go on to win world championships and Olympic competitions. Sadly, Freeth was disqualified from these competitions because he was considered a "professional." After all, he had been paid to give swimming and diving lessons. Never mind that it was the only way he could put food on his table and keep a roof over his head. The disappointment must have been overwhelming for the man who was called the best swimmer and diver in the world by his friend and protégé, Olympic Gold Medalist Duke Kahanamoku.

Freeth's fame as the trainer of champions spread. San Diego's movers and shakers hoped to emulate the LAAC's successes by starting their own "San Diego Rowing Club." One way to accomplish this was to hire the amazing George Freeth away from the L. A. Athletic Club and have him take charge of the Rowing Club's swim program. The job must have paid well, for Freeth accepted the position and moved to San Diego. Reportedly, he transformed the Rowing Club's aquatics into a winning program within the first year of his employment. But when the Rowing Club fell on hard times a short time later, they were forced to let him go.

Despite so many major successes, Freeth found himself unemployed. His financial situation was dire. With little other choice, he took a "land job." Working at the San Diego Cycle and Arms Company in downtown San Diego, he moved into a small room at the Southern Hotel. To supplement his income and continue his love affair with water sports, he worked as a swimming instructor and pool supervisor on Coronado Island during the busy summer months.

He hated his sales job, but times were tough, and the economy was slow. The "Great War" raged on in Europe, and American servicemen were losing their lives. Then as now, San Diego was a military town. Soldiers stationed there flocked to the ocean on their days off, swimming in the all-too-often dangerous surf at Ocean Beach. As drownings soared to record numbers, local officials realized that, like their beach city neighbors to the north, they needed a team of professionally trained lifeguards. At last, George Freeth was back at the beach training San Diego's lifeguards and demonstrating his famous surfing skills.

Author F. Scott Fitzgerald once said, "Show me a hero and I'll write you a tragedy." Unfortunately, the amazing story of George Freeth, a true hero, lives up to Fitzgerald's ominous prediction.

In 1918 the "Spanish influenza" struck America with the ferocity of Thor's hammer. Worldwide, the epidemic claimed over 20 million lives. Meanwhile, San Diego was particularly hard-hit. It's believed that servicemen returning from the war overseas brought the virus with them. Unfortunately, Freeth lived in an inexpensive apartment building which was filled with soldiers.

In early 1919, the surfer from Hawaii who had survived raging storms and deadly rip currents fell victim to the influenza. The virile George Freeth fought with all his strength, finally succumbing on April 7, 1919, at the age of 35. His ashes were returned to Hawaii, where he was buried in the Oahu Cemetery, a stone's throw away from his beloved ocean.

Today, a bronze bust of George Freeth, the "Father of California Surfing" and the "Father of Lifeguarding," graces the Redondo Beach Pier. It's a tribute to his surfing prowess and tireless efforts to create the Redondo Beach Lifesaving Corps, the seaside resort's first lifeguard team. Visiting surfers often drape the statue with flower leis, to pay homage to one of California's forgotten heroes.

Orange County

CONSTANCE HANSTEDT

Curbside, Ronald Reagan Airport

It's three in the afternoon
as the taxi tucks its yellow hull
between a limousine and busload
of boys in matching striped jerseys,
soccer players, I imagine.
They are all white teeth and big eyes
descending two at a time, becoming
a hive abuzz on the curb.

Your ankle looks worse,
my daughter says and I nod,
hesitant of hobbling on crutches
behind sturdy legs of team "Fusion."
What happened? our driver asks,
her brows twin braids of shadow.
I tell her everything: the steps at
Arlington, the mist above headstones,
the distraction of parallel lines.
My daughter laughs lightly, our mutual
tiredness like a vast gray sea.

The driver raises her thin wrist
to the rearview mirror and unclips
a golden angel. *Your protector,*
she says as its cobalt beaded skirt
fans from her hand to mine.
I smile at the blessing in the sunlight
even though I've never believed in
angels. Now mine is this Latina,
weathered cheeks, chapped lips,
voice smooth as water over stone.

Tri-Valley

MARK OWENS *WATCHED THE SMOKE* from the Camp fire in his rear-view mirror. *One more house,* he thought. *Just one more and I'll get the hell out of Dodge.*

His watch showed 3:15 p.m. on November 8th. He already had six laptops with their AC power bricks. Just one more, at $75 each, and he could be in Sacramento by 7 p.m., hook up with the dealer and get enough Oxycontin to last for a few weeks.

The laptops would have burned up in the fire if I hadn't taken them, he rationalized.

The withdrawal anxiety was building; he could feel his skin stretching. An emergency dose in the truck would buy him about six hours of relief.

A large, well-maintained rancher with a long driveway off the main road caught his eye. He positioned the old pickup so that it pointed away from the house, got out, stretched, and walked to the front door. The police had been through the neighborhood a couple of hours earlier. Everyone should have evacuated but, just to be sure, he banged on the front door and yelled, "security."

FIREBREAK
Robert Poirier

He could see movement inside. *Damn,* he thought. *The house should've been empty.*

As Owens turned to leave, he caught movement in the window next to the door. He peered inside and saw an older woman moving away from the door. "Lady," he shouted. "That fire will be here in a couple of hours. You need to get out of here now!"

She turned to look at him, then turned back and continued to move away from the door until she disappeared from view.

"Crap," he said aloud. "I can't leave her here."

The door was unlocked, so Owens walked cautiously into the house in the direction she had gone. "Lady," he said firmly. "I can only stay for a few minutes. I'll help you get in your car, and we'll both leave."

She was sitting in a wheelchair near an open window in the back of the house, holding a black M1911 pistol pointed at his chest.

"Whoa," he said quickly while backing up. "I don't want any trouble. I'll go out the same way I came in."

As he backed out, he noticed a light-blue cord attached to the pistol going out the open window.

He smiled. "Sherlock Holmes and the Problem with Thor bridge," he said.

"Of Thor Bridge," she corrected, emphasizing the word "of."

"Whatever," he said. "My question is, why are you doing this?"

She kept the pistol pointed at his chest. "Doesn't matter," she said evenly. "You have no business here. Leave my house now, please."

"Look, lady," he persisted. "I don't care what you do. But that's a military-style M1911A1 .45 caliber, semi-automatic pistol with three safety features. I can see you have one safety engaged. If I tell you where all the safeties are, will you give me any money you have lying around? It doesn't look like you're going to need it."

She looked at him carefully. "My handbag is on the kitchen counter," she said.

Owens retrieved the handbag and handed it to her. She put the pistol in her lap and rummaged through the bag before proffering several bills.

"Thank you," he said as he took the money. "You have the firing grip safety engaged. The thumb safety only works if the hammer is cocked. Those are the other two safeties. I can see the hammer is not cocked, so the pistol will not fire. I suspect you haven't chambered a round."

She looked at the pistol, cocked the hammer, pointed it at the open window, and pulled the trigger. Owens flinched from the explosion. He took a step forward, swept the pistol from her hand, and engaged the thumb safety.

He carefully wiped the weapon clean and placed it on a table near the entrance to the room.

"It's all yours," he said. "Cocked and locked. Take off the thumb safety, grip the handle, and point it at what you want to kill."

He looked at his watch. He had been in the house for eight minutes. There was still time to get to Sacramento without using his last dose.

"It's none of my business," he said. "But I grew up in Chico and worked with wildfire containment teams while I was going to college. You'll lose the outbuildings, but the main house is probably defensible from the fire."

She paused for a few moments while studying his face. "My nephew left me here early this morning because I told him I was going to change my will and leave my house and money to the ASPCA," she explained. "I thought he was successful and didn't need the money or my life insurance payoff. Apparently, my finances have some irregularities that could ruin him if they were exposed. Something to do with the way the mortgage papers are signed meant I couldn't give away the house. Before he left, he cut the landline and took my cell phone and the car keys."

"The fire would destroy anything I wrote down. I figured I would shoot myself in the head, the gun would end up in the well, and the fire would destroy any evidence. The investigators would see a hole in my head, and, without a gun, the insurance company would claim it was a suspicious death and hold up any payments."

"Great plan," Owens agreed. "But to me, it would make more sense to protect the house and survive to spite your nephew. It would be a case of 'Success was the best revenge.'"

"Is the best revenge," she said, emphasizing the word "is."

"I have a plan," he said. "I'll stay for an hour and prep the house. If it doesn't look like it will work, I'll get the hell out of here, and you can go back to the Thor Bridge plan."

She thought for a moment. "Agreed," she said. "What's your plan?"

"Let me get my dog out of the truck," he said. "Then, I'll check out the property and tell you what I have in mind."

He brought a graying Irish Setter into the house. "This is Eleanor Rigby," he said. "She has been the only one to stick with me for the past couple of years as my life unraveled from opioid addiction."

The dog padded over to the woman and put her head in the woman's lap.

"What a wonderful dog," she said as she stroked the dog's head and back.

Owens was back in the house in a few minutes.

"Do you have a pump to drain the pool, a generator, and some hoses and fittings?"

"The pump and generator are in the tool shed near the pool," she replied. "There should be gasoline and hoses there also."

The large tool shed was well-organized. Owens assembled all the hoses and used an extension ladder to carry the male end of the longest hose up to the roof, positioning it at the center of the ridge. He nailed a small board over the hose to keep it in place.

He selected two oscillating lawn sprinklers, a hose splitter, and several male and female couplings from a large Rubbermaid container. It took about 15 minutes to assemble the sprinkler layout on the roof and turn the output valves on the hose splitter to the off position.

He attached a hose to the pump input and placed the other end into the middle of the pool. The output of the pump was attached to the rooftop hose.

The pump was old but powerful. The roof hose system charged as soon as Owens started the Honda 2000-watt generator and plugged the pump power cord into it.

Owens climbed back on the roof, where he opened one of the hose splitter valves and positioned the attached oscillating sprinkler, so it swept half of the roof with an overspray of about 10 percent. He repeated the process with the adjustment of the second sprinkler. The pump was powerful enough to cover the entire roof area with overspray on all four sides.

By now, it was dusk. The approaching flames, which Owens judged to be about a mile away, and spread across the horizon as far as he could see, projected a yellow light on everything. He spent the last few minutes of the hour using the chain saw to level and throw aside any flammable bushes around the perimeter of the house.

When he went inside, the woman was waiting with sandwiches and a thermos of coffee.

> **"If it doesn't look like it will work, I'll get the hell out of here, and you can go back to the Thor Bridge plan."**

"You still have time to leave," she said as she handed him a quart-sized plastic baggie packed with bills. "I had $750 in a wall safe. Take the money and go. I've lived here for almost 50 years, and I don't have the time or energy to start over."

Owens looked at her for a moment, then put the baggie containing the money inside his shirt.

"If it's okay with you, I would like to stay and keep you company," he said. "I was tagged by an IED while a Marine in Southern Afghanistan and got hooked on opioids while recovering. Helping you is the first good thing I've done in a long time. Let's have something to eat, and I'll tell you the rest of my plan."

While Owens ate, the woman wheeled into the downstairs bathroom and came back with a CVS pharmacy pill bottle. She poured the contents, a dozen round pills imprinted with "512," into a small plastic baggie.

"These are Oxycodone tablets leftover from my hip replacement surgery last year," she said.

They aren't as strong as my regular dose, but they will do, Owens thought. He put the baggie with the pills into the larger baggie containing the money.

After a quick food break, Owens took several brown paper grocery bags out to his truck. He retrieved his emergency dose and then put all the laptops he had stolen into the paper bags, carried them down to the main road, and threw the bags into the bushes. *No reason to be labeled a thief*, he thought.

The wall of flames, spurred on by the high winds, was about three football fields from the house and approaching quickly. The grey smoke was like a thick, choking tule fog as he made his way back to the tool shed. He picked up a heavy canvas tarp and spread it out on the surface of the pool, thoroughly soaking it. Back inside, he picked the woman up from the wheelchair, carried her to the shallow end of the pool, and walked in.

They both gasped from the shock of the cold water. Eleanor was sitting near the tool shed, watching him put the woman in the pool.

"I'm going back for Eleanor."

"Eleanor, come puppy," he called. The dog decided against the water, ran to the tool shed, and started burrowing under it.

By now, the wall of flames was a few hundred yards away. The sky was black, and the swarming, burning embers were falling around him. He could feel the intense heat as he entered the shallow end and pulled the woman toward the center of the pool. When they were deep enough so that his head was just above the water, he pulled the woman close to him so she could keep her head at his level. They were under the center of the tarp, where he could raise his hand slightly and create an air pocket.

The flames roared over them louder than the helicopters that carried him into combat in Afghanistan

The flames roared over them louder than the helicopters that carried him into combat in Afghanistan. The heat penetrated the heavy tarp. He ducked them both underwater every few seconds, then came up for air by raising the tarp. The noise, smoke, and heat died down after 15 minutes. They stayed in the pool for another few minutes; then he lifted the tarp so they could see the house.

"It's still standing," he said, his teeth chattering from the cold.

He picked her up, stumbled back into the house, and carried her to her bedroom, where he removed her clothes and wrapped her in blankets. He started a fire in the living room fireplace, carried her down, and placed her in the wheelchair in front of it.

"You've seen me naked," she said, looking up at him. "You should probably tell me your name."

"Owens," he said. "My name is Mark Owens,"

"I'm Teresa Hardy," she said as she offered her hand. "Nice to meet you, Mark. My late husband was about your size. His clothes are in the bedroom closet."

When Owens, dry and dressed in ironed Wrangler jeans and shirt, looked outside, his truck was a charred hulk with flames pouring from the windows. The generator and pump were still working, and water was cascading off the roof. The outbuildings, including the tool shed where Eleanor had hidden, were burnt nearly to the ground. Tears came to his eyes when he thought about her and how frightened she must have been.

An hour after he had positioned the woman near the fire, Owens noticed a blue flashing light in the driveway. A few seconds later, he could see a sheriff's deputy knocking on the door. The woman wheeled to the door and opened it.

"Hello, Ma'am," the deputy said. "Your nephew asked me to check on the house. He said you had already evacuated, but I noticed smoke coming from the chimney." He looked around the inside of the house and noticed Owens standing by the fireplace. The deputy put his hand on his service weapon in his hip holster and released the holster lock with his index finger.

He stared at Owens, who stood with his back to the fireplace and his arms outstretched on the mantel. "That burned-out Chevy stepside in the driveway fits the description of a truck belonging to a possible looter seen three hours ago a couple of towns away."

"Must be a case of mistaken identity, deputy," she said. "Mister Owens has been here helping me save my house since my nephew left me to die at 10 o'clock this morning."

Teresa Hardy started to cry as soon as the deputy left. She was interrupted by a scratching at the front door. Eleanor, her fur badly singed, came in and immediately went to the woman and put her head in her lap.

"Mark, why don't you and Eleanor stay with me for a few days?" she said. "I worked at the Sutter Health Outreach Clinic in Chico before I retired. I know a doctor who can work with your opioid issues, and you can borrow my car to make any VA appointments."

Owens knelt beside the chair and put his arm around the woman. "I think this is the start of a beautiful friendship."

"Beginning of a beautiful friendship," she corrected, emphasizing the word "beginning" as she smiled at him.

Mt. Diablo

HIS NAME *WAS ANGEL,* an incongruous name for one so volatile. Having Angel in my class was like trying to manage a ticking time bomb that might go off, without warning, at any moment. The fact that he was only four did not diminish his potential for destruction. He was stocky and strong and capable of hurling a toy truck at someone's head with deadly accuracy. The emotions that tossed him around like a cork in a whirlpool held us all hostage. Yet, between storms, he was a charming, little boy. The problem was, no one knew when a storm would hit, not even Angel.

I could tell what kind of morning we were going to have the moment his school bus arrived. Sometimes, he emerged all smiles, eager to start the day. On other mornings, he raged. As the bus doors opened, his screams reverberated across the schoolyard—an auditory assault. All the expert behavioral training in the world could not diffuse that rage. Rational appeals were useless. "Tough love" only fueled the fire. Angel had experienced more "tough love" in his four years than most people experience in a lifetime.

ANGEL SOUP
Pamela Heck

I soon learned that a calm, compassionate approach was the best means of bringing out the "angel" within. Red faced and bawling, he hid behind doors or crawled into a corner of the bathroom. I sat near him to commiserate, "Oh, Angel, I see you are so sad today; so angry today. I think you need a hug."

That worked, maybe not immediately, but soon. A little empathy, a hug and some quiet time with a favorite toy worked wonders. I acknowledged his pain and he was satisfied.

Still, dealing with Angel was a challenge. The room reverberated with a different energy when he was present. He was a lightning-rod. Despite an element of danger, the other children sought him out—often with unwanted results. He was the alpha dog in the pack, the strongest, the most powerful. He was, also, just a little boy confounded by emotions over which he had little control.

Despite his rages, and the energy I expended keeping Angel contained, I was fond of him and tried my best to help. I did it for Angel, of course, but there was a selfish side to this as well. When he was calm and controlled, the whole class ran like a well-oiled machine instead of a jalopy with hiccups and a propensity to backfire.

Providing structure and positive reinforcers helped. And, although it is rarely verbalized, I've found that the caring factor has a transformative effect in the classroom. I cared. Still, all my training and all my caring had not prepared me for the amazing, calming effect of soup.

Angel loved soup. He ate it every day for lunch. Now, I'm not talking the hearty vegetable sort packed full of vitamins and minerals. I'm talking sodium-soaked ramen. Angel would eat no other. I learned to pick my battles, and the calming effect of that brew more than made up for its nutritional deficiencies.

Occasionally, Angel's mother ran out of the preferred fare creating a lunchtime drama of mega proportions. To head off any such future emergencies, I purchased a giant, family pack of ramen at the supermarket and kept it in a cupboard at school. I now had an endless supply of soup, but there was a problem. It needed to be cooked—my job. So, after handwashing, my classroom assistants settled the other students in their places, poking straws into leaky juice boxes and opening the packaging on cheese sticks and yogurt cups and a host of other goodies, all challenging for adults to open and impossible for children.

During that time, Angel followed me around the kitchen like a puppy. He wanted to help. I shuddered. A hot stove, boiling soup and Angel—could that possibly be a good combination? Nevertheless, I decided to give it a try.

The routine never varied. First, Angel carried a small, blue, preschool chair into the kitchen, placed it close to the stove, and stood on it. Right away, we were breaking the "no-standing-on-chairs" rule. Next, I put a pot on the stove and filled a measuring cup with water. Angel poured the water into the pot. After turning on the burner, I opened the bag of noodles and removed the flavor packet. Angel dropped the noodles into the pan. I opened the flavor packet; he shook it into the brew. We took turns stirring until the mix started to boil, practicing our counting to make the time pass more quickly. Once bubbles formed, I let Angel push the timer button on the back of the stove...poke, poke, poke...until the timer read one minute and thirty seconds. At that point, he retired to the lunch table to lay out his sandwich, his juice, and his fruit cup. Soup was on the way! The order never varied and we both came to appreciate the unwavering consistency of the task.

As he stood next to that burner, spoon in hand, I sometimes wondered what my supervisor would say if she happened to surprise me, and my most unpredictable student, laboring together over a hot stove. It was intuition and my unwavering belief that, "sometimes you have to take chances," that put us there. In the six months that Angel and I cooked together, he was unfailingly cooperative. For ten minutes, every day, I was all his. For ten minutes, every day, he could absolutely predict what would happen and it was good. Cooking made a bad day bearable, and a great day even better. I never saw Angel more relaxed than when we were making soup.

Soon other children wanted some. We made a double batch. Angel proudly passed out small portions to his classmates. He became the purveyor of desirable goods and—more importantly—a friend.

Once everyone was eating, I read aloud about Thomas the train. Sometimes the stories featured Henry, sometimes Gordon, but that was as much variety as Angel allowed. Soup and stories—a combination to soothe the savage beast.

During my long career in teaching, I have been called upon to remediate a host of problem behaviors. There are things they teach you in school that help. Most of what works is learned on the job. Structure, positive reinforcement, picture schedules and social stories all help. But here's my advice—when nothing else works, try soup.

Redwood Writers

Concrete Love, photo by Monique Richardson, Tri Valley

IT WAS *ON A NIGHT LIKE THIS* that he passed away. It was a heart attack, they said, which didn't surprise me, the way he smoked, lighting a cigarette with a cigarette. You'd think he'd know better, as smart as he was, but it was the one habit he acquired in the Navy he never could free himself of.

At the time, I was stationed at Fort Irwin and was notified by the battalion's Staff Duty Officer. He had received a Red Cross notification and came to my quarters to inform me of my father's death. He said that AER could help me get back to Oklahoma to be with my family if I wanted, but I declined. Oklahoma had been home growing up, but it wasn't anymore. I had my memories and that was enough.

A BIG SPOON DAY

John Garner

Among them is the day my father gave me the book. I recall it now during the routine I perform before a game to calm my spirit and align my thinking. It's the heavy silence that fills the stadium and the football field stretching out before me that, like some gravitational force, pulls me back to the Saturday in 1958 when we were among the 60,000 crazed fans sardined into Memorial Stadium, cheering wildly as Prentice Gautt and Wahoo McDaniel and the rest of the Sooner team steamrolled Nebraska 47-0.

It's a time in which I no longer dwell but visit often; a time in which I hated my father as much as I loved him. I hated him when he spanked me fiercely and, afterward, set me adrift in a sea of silence. But I loved him just as fiercely on those crisp, autumn Saturdays when Oklahoma played at Owen Field and we'd drive to Norman to see the games. We'd wear ashen gray sweatshirts, emblazoned with red lettering on their front that declared our allegiance to the university and its football team.

Afterward, we'd go to the Dairy Queen and consume foot-long hot dogs, smothered in chili and washed down by strawberry milkshakes that, when drawn up through two straws, chilled the back of our throats. It was there, bathed in florescent light, that we connected. There among the gleaming chrome and red vinyl that my father spoke the one language that spanned the ever-widening gap separating us: football. It was a language with which he was articulate and could speak easily without aid of a slide rule—a subject that, like any conundrum involving mathematics, made him smile.

But that too, the smile, was a conundrum itself as it appeared infrequently.

The games, though, were a thing of beauty, a kind of elegant geometry played out on a canvas of green, against a backdrop of spectators clad in red and white who, when considered as a whole and in the changing light, looked like the dappled brush strokes of an Impressionist painting. The Saturdays, themselves, especially in the fourth quarter, were masterpieces of honey-colored light that angled in from the west and cast long shadows across the lush, green field. Even the gray days whose skies were swollen, and slung low seemed like paintings in which the stadium and its occupants were dwarfed by the impending fury roiling overhead.

As was our ritual, we'd arrived early and were among the few who, with some reverence, watched the great Bud Wilkinson stroll over the playing field, taking in the length of the grass, the gentle slope at midfield, and the direction the wind blew. Thinking back upon it now, I wonder if, in that serene lull before the stadium filled and pulsed with manic energy, if in that moment of quiet introspection, Oklahoma's head coach had been visualizing different situations in the game and developing strategies for them—mentally planning ahead for those times he had only seconds to make critical tactical decisions.

Probably. It's what I do before the teams and spectators arrive, before the stadium lights power up to full brilliance and burn a hole into the darkness. It's what I've always done in the serene lull before a game. That and utter a simple prayer to not fail my team.

But on that Saturday that Oklahoma crushed Nebraska, my father pushed a crumpled grocery bag across the table to me and said, "Here, this is for you."

I was perplexed. A gift?, I thought. My father rarely gave me gifts, and when he did, it was routinely a twenty-dollar bill stuffed into an unsigned card. But given the package's shape and size, I knew immediately that whatever was concealed in the grocery bag wasn't a card, so there probably was no money either. I was disappointed as I could have used the twenty dollars to buy some books.

Setting aside my milkshake, I accepted the package which, from the way my father had compressed the grocery bag to the shape of its contents, I gathered held a book.

"Go ahead," he encouraged, "Open it."

He was animated which puzzled me. What was the occasion that he would give me a gift? Slowly I peeled back the wrinkled brown paper and reached into the bag and clutched what felt like a book. Pulling it out into the white light of the Dairy Queen, I saw that it was red and hardbound, but I saw no title as it was upside down. I fretted that it was another book about dinosaurs. I liked dinosaurs. They were monsters, and they were frightening and, at the same, fascinating. I liked to be frightened and fascinated.

But more than dinosaurs, more than monsters, I liked space invaders. I was as much a fan of the grainy sci-fi movies shown on TV each Saturday night after the news, as I was of the football games broadcast during the afternoon when Oklahoma didn't play at home. My favorite sci-fi movies were *The Day the Earth Stood Still* and *The Thing from Another Planet*, so I hoped that this latest addition to my expanding library was about science fiction, and not science fact.

> *I was perplexed. A gift? My father rarely gave me gifts, and when he did, it was routinely a $20 bill stuffed into an unsigned card.*

But when I looked up from the book, I was jolted from my reverie. My father was smiling. Not a small smile that wrinkled his cheeks, but a big, broad smile that turned up his lips and revealed straight, white teeth. I was shocked. My father was elated. "What do you think?" he asked almost breathlessly as he leaned forward and flipped the book over in my hands.

"It's a book," I replied.

"Yes," my father agreed enthusiastically. "But not just any book. Look at the title." He pointed to the book's cover.

I looked down. There on the front cover was a diagram of a goal post. Between the uprights was printed the book's title: Modern Defensive Football. On the title page was printed the authors' names: Gomer Jones and Charles (Bud) Wilkinson.

I was dumbfounded.

My father had bought me, an eight-year old, a book about football. "What do I do with it?" I asked.

The subject of the book looked as complex as the engineering books my father had stacked on the floor about the drafting table where he worked, often all night, doggedly pursuing a solution to a problem. He was an engineer, and he was brilliant. Not Einstein brilliant, but close. Very close. Unlike other fathers, my father didn't go to work. The work was brought to him.

"You read it," he said. "That's what you do with a book. You read it. Aunt Georgia said you were playing football at school with the other boys and enjoying it, and you read quite a bit, so I thought you might like a book about football." His expression changed. The smile had vanished as if it had been an illusion wrought by the angle of the overhead lights.

"I do like football," I quickly said then, cautiously, added. "But I don't know anything about it."

I weighed the book in my hands, not sure what the gift meant. I loved football. I loved going to the games with my father, watching them on TV, and playing tackle with the neighborhood kids and those at school as well. But when I saw the disappointment etched in my father's face, I was suddenly afraid that he was upset that I didn't fully understand or appreciate his gift. I was distraught that I had, in my confusion, derailed our time together on this golden Saturday afternoon.

And the Saturdays to follow.

The book I could live without, but not this precious time together. It didn't happen often. Only in the fall. Only during football season. And when it did, it was the sweetest slice of life. Like a bowlful of Aunt Georgia's hot apple pie and melting over it, a slab of cold vanilla ice cream. The two extremes in temperature created a harmonious balance that could only be savored when consumed with a big spoon.

That was what today was like: a big spoon day. That was what every Saturday was like when Oklahoma played at home.

"I'll try," I offered.

Pushing the chili dogs aside to make room for the napkins my father spread out on the table, he retrieved an ink pen from his jacket. "I will help," he said, as he put on his glasses and began to diagram the mechanics of the 5-2 defense. Step-by-step, as if he was designing a bridge to span the distance between us, he explained the mechanics of the "Okie" defense in minute detail while I sat mesmerized, transfixed on the X's and O's he drew onto the napkins.

I didn't understand the illustrations or what he was saying, but I loved listening. I loved hearing about the game that brought us together, so that now, so many years later, beneath the white light that bubbled out into the darkness, I am the coach who strolls over the playing field, taking in the length of the grass, the gentle slope from midfield, and gauging the velocity and direction of the wind.

In the distance, in the parking lot behind the locker rooms in the south end of the field, a yellow school bus parks and disgorges his team onto the tarmac. I walk to the home team locker room and am greeted by my players. They are eager to play. I am eager to coach. Tonight, we play Barstow.

In the locker room, the silence is shattered by the players who talk loudly, excitedly, their voices bouncing off the walls. I find my briefcase and open it to retrieve a piece of gum. My mouth is dry. In the front compartment is a book. It is red and worn. I extract it from the briefcase and open it to the first page in the front matter. I remove the napkins so I can read where, in perfect cursive, my father has written me a note. The ink looks like varicose veins.

"In Oklahoma," it begins, "Sundays belong to God, Saturdays to Bud Wilkinson—and to you and me. I want every day to be a Saturday."

It is signed simply, "Dad."

I gently massage the words to imbue them with life, hoping they will leap from the page and take on human form. I want the words given his voice so I can hear them spoken aloud, rather than read. Their insertion into my life as merely a section of script he authored and confined to the interior of a book is troubling only because of what is missing.

So, I imagine a movie scene in which father and son embrace and, as my finger slowly traces the stroke of his pen, I correct the error by inserting the word "Love" before "Dad." It was the one word never spoken aloud; the one word that would have filled the blank space at the end of a big spoon day.

As I study the inscription in the book and reminisce, a player I had nicknamed "Hollywood" back in the spring because he wore mirrored-sunglasses to practice one day, approaches me with a question. "Coach G," he says, smiling broadly, "You got a minute? I'm still confused about my force responsibility in that defense you installed this week."

"You mean the Okie defense?" I reply.

"Yes, sir, that one."

I smile and close the book, returning it to the briefcase. "Come here," I say, indicating the whiteboard on the locker room's front wall. "I'll diagram it for you."

High Desert

JANICE *WAS HIGHER THAN A KITE.* In fact, she was higher than several kites. She looked down from the peak of the roller coaster at the toy beach below, sunbathers like Barbie dolls, children running after those psychedelic kites, all enjoying the first beautiful Saturday of spring.

This natural high was so much better than the ones her high school friends had gotten from their technicolor drugs so many years ago. In college she had satisfied her curiosity and proven it to herself. That was a secret she had kept from Erick. Yes, she did have a secret. He was wrong. She had secrets he'd never know now.

ROLLER COASTER TO ISTANBUL
Beth Lewis

At forty-eight and a half, Janice had woken up and decided it was finally time to experience that high again. Not the drug induced insanity. No, she had hated that. She broke into a sweat just thinking about it. No, not drugs. This, the rush of falling.

She wondered once, not many days ago, if the rush would be heightened by jumping off a bridge instead of the controlled descent of the roller coaster, but then she remembered Elaine. Her best friend had called, begging her to take a trip back in time, back to their youth, back to the roller coaster. Janice had laughed at her. Silly Elaine, didn't she know it was their kids' turn now?

That was just before Erick's birthday. The day he turned forty-eight. The day he turned.

The ride had ended already. Janice was shocked. She had missed it. Her favorite part of the ride: the downhill curve.

"We have to go again," she told her friend.

"Of course, we do," Elaine replied. "Ice cream first."

"No. Now," Janice said, staring at her friend with frightening intensity.

"OK, now's good," said Elaine, looking at Janice as if she'd just told her she had terminal cancer.

"I missed it. I missed my favorite part. Damned bastard made me miss it again."

Elaine reached over and squeezed Janice's forearm.

Janice smiled at her. "Sorry," she said.

"No problem. But if I don't get my ice cream soon, I'll be crankier than you."

Janice chuckled, grabbed Elaine's arm, and dragged her back to the end of the line. They stood, leaning on the metal pipe rail. Janice sensed Elaine watching her and looked back from the crowd.

"He told me I was too predictable."

"What?!"

Janice chuckled. "Yeah, all those years of trying to be what I thought he wanted and then..."

"Did you tell him that?"

"Sort of."

Janice steeled herself, not wanting to relive the scene, but needing so desperately to purge her doubts.

"It was his birthday, his first birthday with no kids since we had them. I made his favorite cake. At least I thought it was his favorite cake. He looked at me and said, 'Jan, you're so predictable.' I wasn't sure what he meant. I still didn't have a clue. Neither did he. I'd been to Victoria's Secret. He'll never know what he missed."

Elaine grinned.

"He looked me right in the eye and said, 'I can't do this anymore. I'm leaving.' I still didn't understand what he meant. I asked him to explain. Why do I always have to be so damned curious? Why couldn't I have just said, 'Fine. Bye,' and shooed him out the door?"

"Because you loved him," Elaine answered.

Janice nodded. "He told me he was tired of always doing the same things, day in, day out, year after year. Knowing what his cake would be was the last straw. I just stared at him for a minute. Then I exploded. I told him how I always made him the same stupid cake because I thought that's what he wanted. How I drove myself crazy every year looking for a new recipe so I could make his favorite cake over and over and not die of boredom. He laughed at me. He had the unmitigated gall to laugh at me! Like I'd made it up or something!

"All those years! All those stupid boring vacations. I told him how I had always wanted to go to Hawaii, Paris. Hell, where I really wanted to go was Istanbul!" She was shaking her head. "Anniversaries at the same restaurant year after year. All for him. All because that's what I thought he wanted. All because I loved him. What a fool. I'm such an idiot."

Janice blinked back tears. Elaine put a hand on her shoulder and looked her in the eye. "You were faithful. You did what you thought was right."

Janice shook her head. "How could I have been so blind? I thought we were happy. I waited years for God's sake, years for the empty nest. Little did I know."

"You can still enjoy it now," Elaine told her friend. "You can do what you like, go where you like, eat what you want, whenever you want."

"Trying for that ice cream again, aren't you?" Janice teased.

"Sounds like you need it more than I do," Elaine answered.

Janice nodded. Predictable. That's something none of her high school friends would have called her. Steadfast maybe. Faithful yes, Elaine was right about that. But predictable? Never. But that's what she'd become. For him. What an idiot!

Jan was dragged out of her thoughts as Elaine's hand clutched her arm. Jan looked to where her friend pointed. "M...m...m... Matthew?" she breathed. Then she yelled it. "Matthew!"

The man turned and froze in his tracks. She'd know him anywhere. He'd been her friend, her confidante, back in high school. What had happened? He'd gone to college, left her behind. Well, not really behind. Not really left either. She'd gone to college too, lost touch. He'd gone off on his own. She'd come here with Elaine. He hadn't written. Then again, neither had she. Where had the time gone?

Janice said under her breath, "Matthew? Is it really you?"

She pulled Elaine by the hand as they clambered under the bars and zigzagged back through the crowds of people waiting to board the Psycho Psyster. Elaine gave Matthew a hug like a Mack truck. Jan just stared. He was chuckling and smiling like a puppy as always. Jan let him hug her. She tried to hug him back, but she fell apart, sobbing.

Matthew looked at Elaine for an explanation.

"Husband left. Six months ago. Just accepted it," she said.

He nodded, "Know what you mean."

Janice finally regained control. "Sorry, Matt. I'm all better now." She looked in his eyes. "You haven't changed a bit."

He ran his fingers through hair shot through with silver. "Neither have you."

"No, Matt. I've changed a lot," Jan answered.

"But I'm trying to change her back as quickly as possible," Elaine added.

Matthew nodded, still staring at Jan.

"So, Matt, how is it you're here? Didn't you go to Yale and become a lawyer or something?" Elaine asked.

"MIT. Engineer," he corrected her.

"Kids?" Elaine continued.

"Three."

"I wanted three," Janice mumbled.

Matt was still looking at her. "Have any?"

"Two. A boy and a girl."

"I bet they're beautiful."

It was all coming back to Janice—how she'd felt about Matt when they were in high school. It had never come to anything. So many times, Janice had decided she was ready, this was it. She was going to sleep with him. Then she'd end up crying on Elaine's shoulder. Matt didn't think it was right, he didn't want to ruin their friendship, he had just started dating someone. Janice would be convinced that he just wasn't attracted to her. Then he would come looking for her. He had made a mistake. She was the only one for him. But by then she'd started dating someone else, yada, yada, yada.

It had driven Jan crazy. How could one or the other of them want it so badly all the time but never both of them at the same time? Matthew's timing was worse than even Murphy's Law could explain.

Janice suddenly realized the conversation had continued without her.

"She gets off work in an hour," Matt was saying.

"We'd love to meet your daughter," said Elaine, with a smile. "Is your wife here too?"

He shook his head. "I'm not married anymore."

"I'm sorry," Elaine said.

"Don't be. We're still friends. It's been over for ages. We just weren't right for each other. She needed someone more like Mr. Cleaver."

Jan and Elaine gave him question-mark faces.

"Like, we got a condo on Maui. She wanted to go there every year, the same two weeks every year. Can you believe it! The same damn condo. Same beach, same restaurants, even the same God damned grocery store!"

Janice began to laugh uncontrollably. Eventually the fit subsided. Wiping the tears of mirth from her eyes, she said, "I always wanted to go to Hawaii."

"Great!" Matt responded. "You can use my condo. Hell, you can have it. She left me with it. God knows why. She only wanted her two weeks a year."

"It might be fun to go once," Janice replied, "but after that I have a million other places I want to see, and I'm getting a late start in life."

"I always had you pegged as a world traveler, Jan. What happened to hitchhiking to Alaska?"

"College happened. Hell, Erick happened."

Elaine slipped away, whispering to Jan as she left, "Ice cream."

Jan nodded, never taking her eyes off Matt as he spoke.

"I'm going to Turkey in August. Will you come with me?"

Redwood Writers

Sweetie

They'll sell the house now that she's gone
toss the little things she loved
plastic souvenirs
crocheted arm rests
old magazines
chipped teacups.
She raised three kids who flew away
back to peck the seeds thrown to hungry birds
anxious to get their fill.

I will remember her soft grey eyes
sad around the edges
her scuffed brown shoes walking slowly down the sidewalk
the TV glowing in her living room window late at night.

She always called me sweetie,
smoothed the rough edges of my adulthood.
I felt her reach out to hug me
with one simple word

Redwood

JOHN PETRAGLIA

May Morning

On Jasmine Road this Spring morning
yellow forsythia make a fence of wildly spiking tendrils
pastel bushes leafing new growth fill neighboring yards
dogwood limbs float in the air, buoyed by pale pink colors
framed by wine elegant Japanese Maples.

Soft new foliage everywhere
canopy counterpoint, silver and yellow greens
random tulips on a rise a curious distance from the nursery
in a light breeze, cherry blossom petals rain on a roadside hillock
and the ever addictive fragrance of ancient lilacs

Over the stone bridge
bone white shards of wood
jag new perches against the wet bark of a buttonwood tree
dark brown earth, mustard greens surround Thoreau's Assabet
moving beyond its banks, washing the flood plain.

Morning mists linger above a pollen-scummed pond
yellow warblers hide among rose-tipped branches
A pair of red-tailed hawks curve high above a fallow field
Green shoots from a rotting log
shadow small turtles trying for the sun.

Who among us denies life after death?
Let them drive through Concord, Massachusetts
this May morning.

Napa Valley

NORMAN *LIVED ALONE IN A WHITE BUNGALOW* on Elm Street in Napa California. Like others of his generation, the retired schoolteacher had a "bucket list." Though he dreamed of climbing Mt. Kilimanjaro or seeing the Taj Mahal, he lived on Social Security and a small pension. By necessity, his list was local.

On Norman's seventieth birthday, he splurged on a bottle of vintage cabernet sauvignon. He retrieved one of the two Riedel crystal goblets in the cupboard and wiped off the dust. The two had last been used as a pair in celebration of his 50th wedding anniversary. But after Dolores passed away a few years ago, there hadn't been much to celebrate. He extracted the cork, poured a small amount and held the glass to the light. He admired the deep, rich, red color and smiled. He swirled the wine and sniffed the bouquet. He savored a sip and quietly said, "Happy Birthday, Norman."

As he did every birthday, Norman retrieved his bucket list from the desk

WINE IN A BUCKET
Bo Kearns

drawer. Over time he had managed to cross out several items. He stared at one still there: Attend Napa Valley Wine Auction. He leaned back in his chair and pictured himself mingling amongst the rich and famous while sipping Napa's finest. He sighed and shook himself back to reality. The cost of a ticket was well beyond his means. Still, he held out hope.

Days later, as he sat at the kitchen table reading the newspaper, an article caught his eye: "Wine auction seeks volunteers." He scanned the list of opportunities: "Parking attendant, limo driver, crew cleanup," etc. Nothing appealed until he spotted "Assist in the barrel room." His pulse quickened. The barrel room would be the scene of the action. He visualized himself standing with the winemakers, talking about terroir, while surrounded by frenzied bidders in designer pastels raising their paddles on high.

He hastened to the computer and filled out the online application. That night he tossed in his sleep, worried he might not get accepted. No need to feel anxious. The following day he received an email, "Welcome, Volunteer Norman."

The day of the auction, Norman arrived early and joined the other volunteers gathering at the staging area. The men wore the prescribed khaki pants and white shirts, the women sported navy skirts and white blouses.

When the shuttle bus pulled up, they all piled in. Norman sat in the back. He gazed around, noticing how much younger everyone else looked. Lately, that had been the trend no matter where he went, yet it didn't bother him. He found their high energy contagious. The bus lumbered along Highway 29 past rows of lush vines, the June grape clusters still a pale green. He eavesdropped on the conservations of those around him. It seemed that most worked for wineries.

"Our winemaker made a rosé this year. Bad move," said a woman with long red hair.

"He should have stuck to cabs and chardonnay," replied the man seated beside her.

"How's business?" someone else inquired.

"Better than last year," came the reply. A nod of heads provided group confirmation. Norman took a deep breath and smiled. He had managed to maneuver his way into the wine business and was now headed to the biggest event of the season.

The bus pulled up to an old, three-story stone building thick with ivy. The volunteers filed off and headed for the registration table. A bespectacled gray-haired woman located Norman's nametag and handed him a long beige apron with the auction logo emblazoned across the front. "Yours to keep," she said. Norman beamed. He hadn't counted on a gift.

"Report downstairs to the barrel room," the woman said. "Look for Holly. She's your team leader. She'll tell you what to do."

Norman wove his way through the crowd and down the winding staircase to a cavernous room where massive oak barrels lined the rock walls. The sun's rays filtered through the small windows high above, casting a hazy aura over the scene. The air had a pleasant chill. Norman paused to bask in the heady atmosphere.

A young woman in a black cocktail dress, fishnet stockings and high heels stood in the middle of the room. Surrounded by a sea of khaki pants and navy skirts, she held a clipboard with a sheaf of papers. Must be Holly, Norman thought, suspecting honchos got to wear whatever they wanted.

As he joined the group, he heard Holly say to a couple, "You two will be covering Blackbird and Shafer." Norman recognized the names as two of the most respected wineries in the Valley. He could hardly wait to find out where he would be stationed.

The next volunteer stepped forward. "Are you sure you registered," Holly asked as she scanned her list.

"Positive," the man replied. She looked skeptical and checked again.

"I really don't have time to deal with you right now," Holly said, her brow furrowed. "Chill for a while. I'll see if I can find something for you to do upstairs."

She turned her attention to Norman.

"Name's Norman Norman," he said pointing to his tag.

Holly's eyes flashed. "Hardly amusing. You're holding up the line."

Norman hadn't expected to encounter Nurse Ratched at the wine auction. Tempted to tell her to check her attitude at the door, he kept his cool. He didn't want to risk getting booted upstairs.

"Norman Norman's my name," he said. "My parents were from the Midwest. They liked everything simple, even their children."

Holly shook her head.

"Looks like Opus One for you, Norman Norman."

Norman pumped his fist. He had arrived at the pinnacle of wine snobbery.

"Don't get so excited," Holly said. "Your job is emptying the spit buckets."

Norman froze. Surely he had misheard.

"Make sure there's no overflow," Holly continued. "Wouldn't want our guests to slip and fall."

Before Norman could protest, Holly cut him off.

"Do a good job and next year you'll get to work one of the bid tables." Holly glanced over his shoulder. "Next."

Norman slunk away. He considered sneaking out the back door, but he had committed. At least he wouldn't have to worry about seeing anyone he knew. Those attending lived in a rarified world of private jets, villas, and Monet originals on the wall.

Around the room winemakers stood beside their barrels busy drawing wine from a bunghole. Tasters swirled the liquid in their mouths. They considered the taste. Then they spat into a silver bucket on the table. Norman stood by watching. He remembered Holly's admonition about overflow. Sensing the moment, he grabbed the handles and lifted while hoping he didn't pinch a nerve in his neck. He made his way through the crowd toward the consolidation vat in the corner. He had to be fast. Someone might want to expectorate before he returned.

After several trips, Norman paused to catch his breath. There has to be a better way, he thought. He searched in the storage room and discovered several more large vats. He took them out and placed them strategically around the room. Now, with less travel time, there was no need for so many runners. Norman had worked himself out of a job. Proud of his initiative, he felt entitled to stroll about, sip wine, and pretend to be one of them. But he had to be careful to avoid Holly.

As he strolled past Frank Family Cellars table, he noticed a line of bidders. An attractive woman, her short, dark hair streaked with gray, sat squinting, looking harried as she tried to record bids.

"Can I help?" Norman asked.

"Oh, please," she said. "Holly assigned me to the most popular station. I should have told her I'm dyslexic. I have processing problems."

Norman assessed the situation. As she recorded bids in the ledger, someone needed to update the large bid board on the wall behind her. He seized the moment and mounted the ladder. "I'll take care of the board, you do the rest," he said.

The bidding kicked into high gear. The price for a case of wine accelerated. How terrific! What a great day for Napa, Norman thought. All the money goes to local charities.

"You're doing a great job, Norman," the winemaker called up to him. "When you have time, come down and taste some wine."

About to accept, Norman spotted Holly approaching. He scrunched down, hoping she wouldn't see him.

"Norman, what are you doing up there? You're supposed to be emptying spit buckets." Her hands on her hips, she stood and glared.

"Everything's under control," Norman replied. "Check for yourself."

"Norman's a big help, I couldn't do this on my own. Don't take him away," the dyslexic woman pleaded. Norman suspected that even hardened Holly would be unable to refuse a woman seeking help.

Holly turned and walked off, her high heels clicking in staccato.

Suddenly the ladder beneath Norman shook. The room resonated with the rattle of glasses and crashing objects. Earthquake!

With fear in her eyes, the dyslexic woman clutched the table.

Norman jumped down to console her. "Just a tremor," he said, though sounding unsure.

"Everyone keep calm," came the voice over the loudspeaker. "Welcome to California. Just our usual shaking." The crowd returned to drinking. Norman, about to remount the ladder, felt another, much stronger tremor. And he heard a loud rumble, like that of a freight train gaining speed. He glanced toward the main aisle, and saw a dislodged barrel headed straight for a tall man, busy texting on his cellphone. Norman sprang into action. He bolted across the room, and reminiscent of his former days on the gridiron, he lowered his shoulder, lunged forward, and knocked the man off his feet. The pair sprawled across the floor.

"What the hell?" the man yelled, his arms flailing. Norman scrambled to his feet and helped him up. At the far end, the barrel hit the wall and exploded like a hard-hit piñata. Wine shot into the air and a wave of red rolled over the concrete floor. The man, still grasping his cell phone, turned to Norman. "You saved saved my life," he said. Norman recognized him. He's the owner of the Golden State Warriors, San Francisco's beloved basketball champions. The owner took a card from his wallet and handed it to Norman. "Call my secretary. She'll arrange season tickets for two."

Norman stared at the card with the prominent royal-blue-and-gold logo. He hadn't done anything special. About to protest, Norman looked up to see the owner had moved on. Too bad Dolores wasn't still alive, Norman thought. She loved basketball. He wondered whom he'd ask to go with him. He turned his attention back to the far end. The scene resembled a war zone. People milled about in shock. Norman grabbed white cloths off the tables to wipe up the spill. "You'll be okay," he assured a woman, her yellow dress covered with red blotches. When there was nothing more he could do, he returned to his station.

"You're a hero," the dyslexic woman exclaimed while giving him a hug. He realized he didn't know her name. He glanced at her tag: "Rose," his favorite flower.

"Rose, do you like basketball?"

"I'm not sure. My ex-husband would never take me to a game. He said I wouldn't be able to follow the fast action."

"Don't worry. I'll explain it," Norman said.

✸✸✸

At the end of the long day, Norman returned home. He opened a bottle of cabernet sauvignon, a thank-you gift from an event winemaker. He poured a glass and held it up to the light. He admired the deep red color. He swirled, sniffed, sipped. He detected flavors of ripe plum and blackberry with hints of vanilla and cocoa. He wondered what kind of wine Rose liked. He suspected a crisp sauvignon blanc.

Norman took his bucket list from the desk drawer. He smiled as he crossed through *Attend Napa Valley Wine Auction*. Further down, he crossed out: *Get tickets to see a Warriors game* and *Find a girlfriend*.

Redwood Writers

MARK MEIERDING

Postlude

When you are severed from a habit of love,
you sit in church and see the pairs
in pews ahead—and the transparent threads
that dance between their shoulders:
a tilt of head, an inhalation, answered,
the way branches of one poplar
sway and return under the same wind.
When you are alone, you only take in,
like a woven funnel awaiting the river's fish,
but between these couples
you can watch cat's cradles of call and response.

Later, navigating the social hall,
you notice how suspended mugs of coffee
put buffers between the visitors,
like the protective tires between dock and disquieted hulls.
You search the faces of other singles
and detect behind their eyes a fallen kite—
or is it only a reflection in glazed panes—
and then you walk home.

Redwood Writers

THE NORTH COAST WIND BIT THROUGH HER linen suit as she stood gazing at the Pacific Ocean. It transformed her hair into miniature whips, stinging her face. A group of young tourists dressed for a Southern California beach huddled nearby.

"Why is it so cold?" one asked. "It's May!"

The youngsters piled back into their car and drove off without a glance her way, leaving her alone on the cliff top. She watched the rhythmic pounding of waves on sand, the sound reaching her ear a fraction of a second after the shore took each blow.

If the cliff were more vertical, if the waves were only a leap away, she would probably already be in them. She pictured herself remaining calm as she was sucked under by the current.

How long would it take for the life to leak out of her body, she wondered. Five minutes? Ten? She imagined coming face to face with a cute harbor seal in her last moments.

"Ma'am?"

She turned her head to see a young man with furrowed brow looking at her. He must have hiked up the beach trail. The black pickup truck at end of the pullout must be his.

"Are you alright?" he asked.

Southern, clearly. Military, likely. The posture. The hair. The foresight to have brought a heavy jacket to the Sonoma Coast.

She looked back at the sea mutely, the beautiful sea that gives us life, life we eat, life we pollute.

"Ma'am. Can I help you?"

She turned back to him, seeing the strength and youth aflame in him. How beautiful he was, with the promise of a life ahead of him.

She shook her head.

AT THE CLIFF'S EDGE
Cristina Goulart

"I've had bad days too," he said.

"Have you ever had a bad decade?" she asked.

"No, ma'am, but I've been at the cliff's edge, a few times myself. Will probably be there again."

She was comforted by that, but looked away, embarrassed to be comforted by another's suffering.

"You're shivering," he said.

"Am I?"

"Yes, ma'am."

"I don't feel it."

A gale hit them, unsteadying them both.

"That wind could knock you over the cliff," she said to him. "You should step further away."

"Take your own advice?"

She stayed put.

He kept his gaze on her for a moment, then edged closer to the cliff and looked down.

"You know, you're not making it into the water from here. You're just going to roll and bounce part way down. Break a couple bones maybe."

She was contemplating suicide. He was talking her down. This boy, talking down a stranger, a woman old enough to be his mother. But no, she thought, he wasn't a boy. He was young, but he'd lived. There was a set to his jaw, lines come too early to his eyes.

"Alabama?" she asked.

"Good guess. Fifty miles to the west."

"Mississippi."

He smiled. "Someone out here knows her geography."

"Stationed at Two Rock?" she asked.

"Coast Guard? Heck no, I'm Army," he beamed. "I'm driving down the coast from Oregon on leave. Wanted to be alone."

"They say being alone isn't always the best thing for those of us who tend to the cliff's edge."

He shrugged. "It's quiet when I'm alone."

"In your head, maybe."

He laughed with a snort, which made her smile despite herself.

"May I ask, have you seen combat?"

"Two tours." His eyes hardened, and he looked away, off to the watery horizon.

"You've seen worse than I have. I guess you'd think my life is easy."

He looked back at her. "Oh, I had been at the cliff's edge before I ever went to those deserts. At least in the Army I'm never alone." He shuffled. "That sounded stupid."

"No, it didn't," she said.

"If you haven't been in, you wouldn't know what I mean. Outside it can be lonely, everyone for himself," he said. "Or herself," he added and shot her a glance.

She nodded. "It can feel like running alone on a treadmill, hoping you don't fall off. Not wanting to find out if anyone would help you back up."

He extended his hand. "I'm Shane."

"I'm Nancy," she said, and shook his hand.

"It's fixing to be a pretty sunset."

She smiled at his vernacular.

The sun sank lower, drenching the scattered clouds with pink. The two of them stood together watching the sky, silently grateful, silently taking a step away from the cliff's edge.

Redwood Writers

SOMETHING BIG HAPPENED last May among our hundred-year-old row houses down by the river. It brought us out together.

A fire that started in an oil spill on her kitchen stove burned Señora Rosales' place to the ground. It was horrid, but that's not what I'll remember.

We streamed to the sidewalk across the street, watched some neighbors run in and out of their front doors, dragging out sticks of furniture or carrying boxes of photographs. Mr. Abalon lugged out a huge carpet roll, but once to his gate, he dropped the rug and grabbed his chest. There he stayed. Mrs. Johnson carried brass candlesticks and her granddaughter's painting of Jesus. She wept.

The fire now burst through the Rosales' roof. Distant sirens wailed, but the only help for poor Señora was from Lucky Luce spraying his garden hose around, more on his own roof than on hers. The fire felt hot on my face.

CHARACTER
Tim Jollymore

When *los bomberos* stopped at the tracks blocks away, Señora screamed. We tore our eyes from the fire. She slapped her hands to her cheeks, screamed again, "*Perrito! Dios mío!*" Her pug, Chachalaco, was in the house. "*Discúlpeme, Jesús,*" she cried.

Everyone knew Chacho. He was a little brown barrel on legs and barked like a fat man choking on chicken bones. He grunted like a piglet.

The tall kid who lived past Johnson's stepped up to her and leaned down to her ear. She clasped her hands at her chin, looked up at him, then closed her eyes, saying, "*Por favor, mi hijo, por favor.*"

He strode straight across the street. He lifted Lucky's hose, sprayed his Padres hat, doused his curly hair, and soaked his tee shirt and jeans. He handed Lucky the hose and strode right up that walk. I can still see his straight, bony shoulders moving under his tee as he marched to the Señora's front door.

No one spoke. People stopped running. They set down their loads and waited. Señora Rosales prayed. Flames roared and sirens wailed crescendo.

I was glad we lived in row houses. They were painted or peeling different colors but otherwise were exactly the same. Even in pitch dark, you couldn't get lost in any neighbor's house.

We stood open-mouthed—it seemed like fifty years—waiting. Now, everybody prayed. Then with a groan the kitchen roof buckled. Dining room windows exploded onto the sidewalk. We sucked air. Lucky wet his shoes with the hose.

At the moment fire engines rounded the corner, out comes the kid holding Chacho. He reached back, closed the front door, and walked right to La Señora. Everyone cheered. He held Chacho out to her. "He was hiding under the bed." The pug licked her face furiously, choking and grunting like mad. We all clapped like it had been some kind of performance or something.

That house is gone now, a front tooth knocked from a neighborhood smile. Even little kids still remember that fire. A few adults say it was foolishness to enter a burning house. Others say it was heroism.

The fire's not what I'll remember. It was great for the kid to brave death and carry Chacho out of a burning house though neither his coming out nor going in is what I'll remember.

What I'll see forever are those squared, broad shoulders he carried toward the door. Entering the house, he was all the neighborhood's hope. Coming out, he was everybody's hero.

But what will always make me remember him is that when he came out, he closed the door.

Berkeley

THE HUGE MOON ***ROSE IN THE EASTERN SKY*** over Kauai where my husband and I celebrated our wedding anniversary on a warm February evening. A light breeze scattered clouds across the bright orb. My fingers entwined with Paul's as we walked along the sandy beach after sipping Mai Tais and watching the sunset. I felt just a teeny bit tipsy. Despite the perfect setting and the Mai Tais, I struggled to ignore a vague sense of unease. Full moons unnerved me for no reason in particular. I don't consider myself superstitious, but I do have some exceptions.

Paul and I paused to enjoy the bird's-eye view of the rising moon and the soft caress of the Hawaiian breeze off the ocean. Hand in hand, we meandered back toward our hotel. The beach ended at a rocky cliffside. As we turned onto the hotel grounds, a long, lit staircase framed by columns appeared ahead of us.

"I don't recall seeing that earlier," I said. "I wonder what's up there?"

FULL MOON
Fran Cain

"I don't remember it either. Must have been the Mai Tais." My husband led me to it. Although the entrance was open to the elements, like many lobbies in Hawaii, framed paintings hung on either side of the hallway. We proceeded to walk up the staircase, admiring the artwork. A half-dozen shallow two-step flights separated by landings ended at an elevator door.

"This must go to a parking lot. Or maybe it's a service area." I looked around for signs but there were none. Paul pushed the elevator button. The doors slid open immediately. We looked at each other, then I peeked inside the door looking for some sort of clue.

"Go in," he said.

I saw his dark eyes lit with curiosity.

"Are you sure you want to do this?" I stepped inside, a willing participant in this game.

He followed and pushed the one button. The doors slid closed without a sound. We ascended for a short ride and the doors opened. We stepped out onto a small outdoor patio.

"An overlook for lovers, perhaps?" I said. "Except there's no view of the ocean." The patio should have looked down to the beach, but hemmed in by dense bushes, we couldn't see beyond. Hand-in-hand, we crept around to the back side. I couldn't help feeling that we shouldn't be there, yet there was nothing stopping us. To my surprise, the rear of the patio extended to a long, wide, covered walkway illuminated by low lights.

"Where could it lead?" I considered getting back in the elevator, but now I was enticed. "I have to know," I said.

Paul didn't resist. Maybe the Mai Tais had caused us to throw caution to the wind.

I saw no people, no cars, no parking lot, no buildings. I felt my husband's hand squeeze mine more tightly as we proceeded. In what was left of the light from the sunset, I could see vast open areas on either side of the walkway, some grassy and some dark and overgrown with clumps of brush. The walkway split in two directions. At the intersection sat a large, cross-legged Buddha. Beyond the statue, I could make out a deserted stadium with seats overtaken by vines and weeds.

"This looks like it could have been a sports center," Paul said.

"It's a little creepy, if you ask me," I let go of his hand and grabbed onto his muscular arm for security.

Not a soul, bird or insect stirred. In the silence, darkness closed in. At the next intersection, a sea nymph lit by one of two lamps beckoned us to continue.

At last, a low dark building with no windows materialized ahead of us. Although a few ground level lights illuminated the grassy area along the walkway, low trees obscured the sky, adding to the intrigue.

At the next turn, the walkway finally ended at a huge, dimly lit patio, furnished but empty of people.

"This must be another hotel." I struggled to make sense of this odd property.

A covered porch beyond the patio held displays of large photos. I let go of Paul to get a closer look at pictures of winter ski areas and mountain resorts. Beautiful but obviously not Hawaii. Why were they here?

I followed the porch to a well-lit lobby, completely deserted. Paul poked around looking in the empty offices where people should be.

"Where are the people?" I said.

"I don't know." Paul shrugged. "I'm looking for clues."

Bewildered, I searched the ceiling for signs of security cameras, suspicious we were being recorded. At the rear of the lobby, an open double door led to another, smaller patio. The sound of soft Hawaiian music surrounded us as we stepped through the doors and found ourselves overlooking a dark lake shimmering with the reflection of the full moon overhead. My husband drew me close. Despite the strangeness, I felt bathed in the peace and beauty of the moment.

Yet, at any time someone could appear, asking what we were doing there. Paul must have felt it too.

"We'd better go," he said.

Reluctantly, I followed as we retraced our steps, glowing with the wonder of discovering this place, and feeling a bit of fear that we could be caught trespassing.

★★★

Halfway back, we paused at the sea nymph statue.

"What's that hum?" I said.

"Must be the lighting. Probably an electrical problem," my husband said. "This second lamp isn't working." He pointed to a dead light, then kept walking.

A cool breeze came up, and I heard the rumble of thunder in the distance.

"I hope it doesn't rain."

I turned at the intersection and came face to face with a man.

My heart jumped in my chest.

He towered over me and wore a flowing cape that appeared to be made from feathers.

"Hello," I said, trying to sound natural.

I couldn't make out his features in the dim light. My husband's hand squeezed mine hard. The man held a long staff, or a spear, in one hand, and lifted his other hand to point towards the moon.

"Nice cape," I said, as cheerfully as I could, given the pounding of my heart.

He didn't reply.

My husband started to maneuver me past the man, but he held his arm out as if to stop us.

"Excuse us," my husband said.

The man didn't move. My husband brushed past and pulled me along. I glanced back over my shoulder. The man seemed frozen in position with his arm still out.

"Run," my husband directed.

I struggled to keep up, my sandals flip-flopping against the pavers.

We reached the elevator and my husband pounded the button. The door slid open. I looked behind again to be sure we weren't followed.

"Hurry up." My husband yanked me in and punched the button to close the door.

The elevator descended and the door opened. I grabbed Paul's arm for support and hurried back down the stairs.

No bright light shone from the moon anymore. Fog had moved in and a round shadow appeared where the moon should be. I could hear the sound of waves slapping the pitch-dark beach, and the wind had picked up.

"We should go straight to the lobby and report that guy," I said. "He was weird."

"You're right," Paul said. We rushed towards the main building passing the hotel pool. The lights were on and music wafted from the adjoining bar where we had our cocktails earlier. But it was deserted.

The man didn't move. My husband brushed past and pulled me along. I glanced back over my shoulder. The man seemed frozen with his arm still out.

"What time is it?" I asked.

Paul glanced at his watch.

"It's 9:45. Seems kind of early for everyone to be in for the night, doesn't it?" he asked.

"Yeah. Before we went in that elevator, there were a lot of people at the bar, and a line at the restaurant," I said.

We followed the walkway around the pool, up a double flight of stairs, along a second story veranda, past another bar, also deserted, past a vacant gift shop with doors wide open, and finally into the open-air lobby. The same Hawaiian music played in the softly lit room. The concierge desk was empty. The timeshare desk was empty. The front desk where we had checked in that morning was empty.

"Wow, this place is deserted," I said, stating the obvious. "Maybe I can call someone." I looked around for a nonexistent hotel phone.

"I have the number for the hotel in my contacts." Paul pulled out his iPhone. "I'll try calling."

I shivered in the wind. Paul put his arm around me and pulled me against his warm chest while he waited for the call to go through.

"It's not ringing. It's like its dead." He pressed the end button and looked at the phone. "It's got a full signal, but the call isn't going through." He tried again then put the phone back in his pocket. "Let's go to the room. I should be able to reach the operator or the security office or housekeeping from there. Someone's got to be working."

"This is so weird. Where is everyone? What if we see that guy again?" I said.

"If we see him, just stay behind me," my brave husband said.

He guided me along a lit walkway lined with sculptures of Hawaiian kings and mythical sea monsters. Every few seconds I glanced around looking for the stranger. When we finally reached our room, Paul pulled his key card out of his wallet and waved it in front of the card reader. A red light came on.

"Must be user error," he said.

He waved it again, slower this time. Still the red light glowed.

"Crap." He tried again. No luck. "Do you have your key?"

I fished mine out of my pocket and waved it in front of the reader.

Nothing.

He checked his iPhone. No signal.

"I have the car keys. Let's go to the parking lot," he said. "We should see a security guard or an attendant. If not, we can drive around the property until we get a signal or see a guard."

> *The parking lot overflowed with cars, but no people, and no guards appeared. Paul pressed the unlock button on the fob. Beep-beep. He pulled on the door handle. It wouldn't open.*

"But that means we have to go past that elevator again."

"Come on." He took my arm.

We rounded the bend towards the dark parking lot. When we saw the walkway to the elevator, Paul quickened his pace.

"I'm really scared," I said.

"Shh."

"I'm really scared," I whispered.

The parking lot overflowed with cars, but no people, and no guards appeared. We found our rental, one of many red convertible Camaros. Paul pressed the unlock button on the fob. Beep-beep. He pulled on the door handle. It wouldn't open.

"Crap." He tried again. "Go around and see if the passenger door is open."

I hugged myself as I left his side and went around the car. I pulled the handle.

"Nope."

"Now what do we do?" he said. "There's no one around, the lobby is empty, we can't get into our room, we can't get into our car."

Despite the tropical location, the wind felt almost arctic.

"I need to get warm," I said. "I'm starting to freeze. It was warm when we came out to watch the sunset."

"Everything is open air in Hawaii," he said. "Even the restaurants."

"What happens here when its stormy?" I said, rubbing the goosebumps on my bare arms.

"It's usually really warm in Hawaii, so even if it's stormy, you don't need a jacket or coat."

"Yeah, well, that's not the case now," I said. "I wish I had my ski parka."

"We could get inside the elevator," he said. "I noticed it was warm in there."

"Are you crazy? What about the guy?"

"He must be gone by now," he said.

"Well, I can't stay outside all night. My teeth are chattering," I said. "If that's the only place to get warm, I don't think we have a choice."

Paul led me back to the elevator. Walking up those steps, my heart raced with dread. But I felt colder by the second and needed to get warm.

Before we reached the door, it slid open.

"Come on," Paul said.

The door closed behind us. Warm air filled the dimly lit compartment. He wrapped his arms around me, and we slid gently down to sit on the floor.

✶✶✶

I startled awake. Beside me, Paul snored softly. We must have fallen asleep, but for how long? I shook him gently.

"What time is it?" I pushed my hair back from my face.

He squinted at his watch.

"It says 7:30. We must have been here all night."

"What?" I said, pulling myself to my feet. "Push the button."

He stood and pushed the button.

I expected the door to open, but instead the elevator ascended. It stopped and the door opened. We stepped out onto the little patio and walked around the back side, like we did the night before. Birds chirped and chattered in the warm morning light. People milled about looking at the scenery.

"Good morning," a dark-skinned Hawaiian man wearing a colorful floral shirt with a name tag stood to one side. "How may I direct you this morning?"

"We were here last night right after sunset," Paul said. "There wasn't a soul around."

"I'm so sorry, sir. I would be happy to arrange a tour of our newest timeshare property for you."

101

"Timeshare?" Paul looked at me, and I raised my eyebrows.

"Yes," the man said. "We still have some construction going on, so prices may never be better."

"Maybe another time," I said. "But may I ask a question?"

"Of course." The bellman smiled.

"Last night we ran into an odd man wearing a feathered cape."

"Hmm…" The bellman didn't seem surprised. "Perhaps you mean you met the king."

"The king?" Paul said.

"Yes, sir. We have a sculpture of King Kamehameha wearing a reproduction of the feathered cape he wore when he ruled here. It's right over there." He pointed and we saw the figure in the distance.

"But he moved and tried to block our way," I said. "So, it couldn't have been a statue."

"I see." He frowned. "I have heard tales that he comes alive during the full moon. Legend has it that time stops and he roams the land mourning his troops who died during his attempts to invade Kauai in the 1700s." His face relaxed, and he smiled. "But of course, those stories are just myths." He gave a small bow. "Please excuse me, I see someone has a question." He turned away.

"Paul." I grabbed his arm and pulled him aside. "That must have been him," I said. "King Kamehameha walking the earth during the full moon. Maybe that's why we couldn't find any people and why nothing worked. Do you think it's possible?"

"That's silly," he said. "I don't believe in that stuff. I'm not superstitious."

"I'm not either," I said. "Except when it comes to the full moon."

Mt. Diablo

Terri

She is not particularly pretty

and her nose is a little too strong,

but as the heat and light of an oven

changes a little of this and a little of that

into a delicious dessert,

She smiles.

Redwood Writers

MOST WRITERS ARE IN LOVE WITH THE WRITTEN WORD.

All of those synonyms and antonyms. Beautiful metaphors. The rhymes and rhythms of language. It's all great until you can't remember the word that is on the tip of your tongue. Or your dear friend's name, as he stands next to you waiting to be introduced to someone.

I once had a migraine headache that induced a kind of what's-it-called, aphasia. For a few minutes I struggled to produce the words that were in my head and I soon noticed that the sounds I was emitting were not what I intended. Very scary, to say the least. As the person with whom I was meeting stared at me wide-eyed, I ran out of the room and took the elevator to my building's medical office. Leaning on the intake counter, I struggled to get out the words, "I . . . can't . . . talk." Fortunately, by the time a nurse saw me, it was over. The experience has never been repeated, but the memory remains of how unnerving it was to be unable to communicate.

WHAT'S THAT WORD?
Lenore Hirsch

Recently a dear friend wrote to compliment me on my "self-defecating" humor. That cracked me up. Yes, self-deprecating is a little like acknowledging that the you-know-what has hit the fan and it's your fault.

When a group of upper-end Boomers gets together, there is a constant pause in the conversation while one person is searching for the right term: "You know, that medicine that is good for—you know—that condition that is painful and has to do with inflammation" and everyone else is guessing, "Advil, ibuprofen, Aleve, aspirin." It's like a constant game of charades. Sometimes this situation is funny, but more often, it's just annoying: "You know that movie about two people in some foreign country and one of them is played by what's-his-name." I mean, really. We should all try to think it out in advance and for goodness sake, if you can't be more specific than that, forget about it! Or keep a young person around who knows how you think; perhaps he or she can translate.

Those of you on the younger end of the Baby Boom may not yet have any experience with what I'm talking about. This is your chance to educate yourselves. Take this opportunity to realize what is ahead, party hardy while you can, and lend a hand to your elders.

One thing I've noticed about my own search for missing words is that the harder I try to remember, the less likely it is that the word will pop to the surface. So find some way to shift the conversation or put it off until later. Of course, there is always our invisible friend, Siri. How did we ever manage a dinner conversation without using Google to check facts? So Siri, what are those over-the-counter medications good for inflammation? I tried this and got a list of NSAIDs. Not bad. Just make sure you're in range of Wi-Fi or a cell tower at all times.

Of course, relying on Google does nothing for your embarrassment at being unable to finish your sentence or remember your friend's name. Rather than getting disgruntled and upset—"Damn, why can't I remember this? I'm losing my mind"—just smile and laugh it off. Or say to your friend, "Would you be kind enough to introduce yourself? I'm beat." If your friend can't remember his own name, then you have a serious problem. Otherwise, it just goes with the territory of getting older and we all should forgive each other, laugh, and have another glass of wine.

Napa Valley

Collage by Audrey Kalman, SF/Peninsula.

RANDALL MCNAIR

The Poetry Pandemic of 2020

What if a poem could spread across
the globe like the novel coronavirus,

this stanza getting sneezed into
existence on an airplane, that one

passing hand to hand
via the handshake of old friends

What if, instead of sickness, this world
was faced with a poetry pandemic?

Words like roiling and rollicking
sticking to doorknobs and steering wheels

while sonnets travel from baby to baby
as their nannies wheel them through parks

where couples pass couplets to each other
beneath their blankets

Wouldn't it be great if, instead of burying
our loved ones, we could merely crumple up

the bad poems and toss them into the trash,
crisis averted?

Sure, there is poetry in human suffering,
but imagine for just a second, a world where

humans could live forever, provided a single
poem was spreading mouth to mouth amongst us,

a poem of great wisdom, or wit, or love of life,
or even a poem like this one.

Berkeley

Mustard looking toward Sonoma Mountain photograph, by Shawn Langwell, Redwood

Submit your best work to the
2021 CALIFORNIA WRITERS CLUB LITERARY REVIEW
Submission window announced late August, 2021.
All details at *calwriters.org*

In Canyon, photograph by David A. Rosenthal, East Sierra.